* * * * * * * * * * * *

Ask and You Shall Receive

✳ ✳ ✳ ✳ ✳ ✳ ✳ ✳ ✳ ✳ ✳ ✳

Ask and You Shall Receive

A Fundraising Training Program for Religious Organizations and Projects

Leader Manual

Kim Klein

JOSSEY-BASS
A Wiley Company
San Francisco

Jossey-Bass books and products are available through most bookstores. To contact Jossey-Bass directly, call (888) 378-2537, fax to (800) 605-2665, or visit our website at www.jossey-bass.com.

Substantial discounts on bulk quantities of Jossey-Bass books are available to corporations, professional associations, and other organizations. For details and discount information, contact the special sales department at Jossey-Bass.

 Printed in the United States of America on acid-free, recycled stock that meets or exceeds the minimum GPO and EPA requirements for recycled paper.

Library of Congress Cataloging-in-Publication Data
Klein, Kim.
Ask and you shall receive: a fundraising program for religious organizations and projects: leader manual / Kim Klein.—1st ed.
p. cm.
Includes bibliographical references.
ISBN 0–7879–5130–7 (alk. paper)
1. Church fund raising. I. Title.
BV772.5 .K56 2000
254′.8—dc21

00–09567

PB Printing 10 9 8 7 6 5 4 3 2 1   FIRST EDITION

Contents

* * * * * * * * * * * *

Ask and You Shall Receive

✳   ✳   ✳   ✳   ✳   ✳   ✳   ✳   ✳   ✳   ✳   ✳

Introduction:
Who Is This Book For?

MORE THAN five hundred thousand nonprofit organizations in the United States are classified in the nonprofit taxonomy as "religious." These organizations run the gamut from churches, synagogues, temples, and mosques to the social service agencies, schools, retreat centers, seminaries, outreach programs, and missions that are affiliated with them. In addition to these groups, there are thousands of nonprofit organizations that find information and inspiration for their programs in scriptures and religious literature, even though they may not be affiliated with a specific religious institution. Finally, there are thousands of committees, caucuses, task forces, study groups, and other formations of people who are not incorporated officially as nonprofits but who have important ministries in their neighborhoods and communities.

This book is written for a subset of these hundreds of thousands of organizations: religious groups that have certain attributes in common:

- They have annual budgets of no more than $300,000; for most, the budget is considerably lower.

- Their work is done almost entirely by volunteers, as is their fundraising.

- The same volunteers who lead these organizations will be leading the fundraising training outlined in this book.

- These volunteers don't have a lot of time to learn about fundraising.

Many people ask whether raising money for a religious organization is different from raising money for any nonprofit. The answer is yes and no. In an operational sense, the major differences in nonprofits have much more to do with size than with issues. Strictly in terms of fundraising, a very large Jewish service organization has more in common with a secular United Way than with a small synagogue. A Presbyterian church with several ministers, a day care program, an active overseas mission program, a campus ministry, and a senior outreach effort has much more commonality with a secular multiservice agency than with a rural Presbyterian church led by laypeople. A well-established seminary will find they have the same challenges as a small liberal arts college, whereas a small Buddhist retreat center enjoys many of the same opportunities for fundraising as an ecology center with a live-in staff, interns, and work-study programs.

However, there are some important differences between religious and secular groups that make fundraising both harder and easier for religious groups. What makes it harder is a perception that it is easy to raise money for a religious cause ("Well, you have God and guilt on your side. What else could you need?" or "People give to religious causes in order to get into Heaven" are comments often heard). This perception trivializes a religious person's motives for giving and assumes that all religious people believe in a God who rewards and punishes.

A second difficulty arises because of the separation of church and state. Corporations and foundations are leery of giving to religious causes, and federated funds rarely include religious organizations. Although religious institutions sometimes do receive government contracts to provide social services, the government agency administering the contract must make sure there is a "firewall" between the social service and the rest of the work of the religious institution.

On the other hand, what makes fundraising easier is a long tradition of giving to religious institutions. To be asked for money during a religious service is expected, and to be asked week after week is also commonplace. Further, religious institutions are seen as permanent and stable. They are perceived to be an integral part of a healthy community and tend to command respect even from those who may disagree with them.

Finally, research shows that most givers to all nonprofits describe themselves as "religious or spiritual," so religious institutions have access to the most thoughtful and generous givers. Of course, thousands of secular groups have religious roots, so religion and spirituality play an immense role in all philanthropy.

This book is written for the smaller end of the income-needing spectrum; it is also aimed at those many hybrid religious organizations that reflect an ecumenical spirit and a belief that all true seekers will find God on any number of roads and paths. It is written for people who are creating you may from time to time want a refresher on one session or another, in which case you could use a session alone. The beginner or the volunteer with some experience in fundraising but no formal training will find that each session builds on the one before; they are designed to be taught together.

How to Use This Manual: Notes for Leaders

WELCOME TO an exciting adventure: teaching your peers how to raise money! The notes in this section help you do the best job you can. The training design, the exercises, and the information presented here are taken from years of training that I have provided to thousands of groups and individuals. The manual has been reviewed by people who are not professional fundraisers, to help eliminate jargon or strategies that are too difficult to teach in this format, and to make sure that the level is appropriate for beginning students of fundraising.

For more information, a Bibliography at the end of the participant manual as well as this leader's manual include a number of websites that have a lot of free information about fundraising. My sincere hope is that this material and the resources provided will give you the confidence you need to undertake this important task.

My fundamental beliefs, which inform this curriculum, are that grassroots fundraising—the philosophy, the strategies, and the practice—is something that people in religious organizations know far more about than they realize, and that it can be taught by people who are not experts. In other words, it does not require expertise to teach the content of this program to people who have experience being part of an organization—and experience in giving away some of their own money.

MY ASSUMPTIONS ABOUT YOU, THE LEADER

The following are my assumptions about you as the leader of this training:

- You do not know any more about fundraising than the people in the group you are working with. If you do, that will help you in preparing for each session, but it is not required. You give away some of your money, and how much you give is informed (in part at least) by the guidelines of your religious tradition. As such, you know what it is like to make choices about your donations and to have to say no to some causes, and you know what it is like to be asked for money. You may have done some fundraising already, but that is not required to lead this course.

• You have led Sunday School classes, workshops, or seminars, or taught adults in some other way and are comfortable leading a group.

• You are willing to spend the time to lead this course and to find the time to prepare for it. Generally, it will take you thirty minutes to prepare for each hour that you teach. Preparation includes becoming familiar with the material in your manual and the participant's manual, making sure you understand the exercises and, occasionally, photocopying handouts or preparing something specific to your group ahead of time.

• You are deeply committed to a religious or spiritual organization and want that organization to raise money effectively. This probably means that you want it to raise more money, but it also means that you want your fundraising efforts to be efficient, planned, and strategic so that your organization does not have to work harder to make more money.

MY ASSUMPTIONS ABOUT WHOM YOU ARE TEACHING

You are working with a group of seven to twenty adults who together are involved in one project or organization. The material is designed to bring basic fundraising knowledge to as many people in one organization as can attend the sessions. It is an inexpensive and fairly easy way to ground yourselves in the basics of fundraising and learn how you can use the most common fundraising strategies. You can modify this material to work with people in one group who come from a few different organizations, but it would be best not to have more than four groups represented.

If you have fewer than seven adults, all of you may want to take turns presenting a session; as well, turning the presentation of any one session over to someone else in the group is always an option. If your group is larger than twenty but fewer than thirty, you could find a co-leader to help you debrief exercises, write on the flipchart, and prepare some of the sessions. If your group has more than thirty members, you will want to divide it in two.

A final assumption is that the people who sign up for this course are committed to coming to each session if they possibly can. Participants should not be allowed to drop in on sessions as they desire. They are expected to come on time, and new people allowed to join the course after it has begun must make some arrangement to get caught up on what has been covered, particularly in the opening sessions. However, working with volunteers means that people will miss sessions from time to time. Therefore, the beginning of each session is devoted to reviewing the previous one, answering lingering questions, and bringing up to speed anyone who missed the session.

HOW EACH SESSION IS DESIGNED

Each session is designed to last about sixty to ninety minutes. Some could take as long as two hours. The length of time depends in part on how you structure the sessions: if you have a number of people who miss sessions and need to be brought up to date, or if you spend a lot of time on review or invite guest speakers, your sessions will obviously be longer. All of the sessions have exercises, and all raise discussion topics that could take more than one hour to cover, so if your Sunday school class or study group sessions generally last ninety minutes, you can give people a ten-minute break halfway through and allow a few more minutes on each exercise, or let a particularly intense or interesting discussion continue past the time recommended. Though sessions are not designed to be rushed, they are full. If you wish to start your session with a prayer or meditation, you need to factor that into your time planning, and you should also allow five to ten minutes for evaluation at the end of the session.

The content for the session is first introduced, followed by an opening exercise whose purpose is to get people focused and interested in the topic. After the opening exercise, there is a presentation about the topic, which is sometimes didactic and sometimes calls for group discussion. There are usually two to four more exercises of various kinds interspersed with presentation for the rest of the session. The session ends with a wrap-up, usually of key learnings, an evaluation, and a one- or two-sentence introduction to the next session. If you wish to end the session with a prayer or meditation, allow two or three minutes to do so.

Each chapter (session) of the leader's manual begins with an outline of the session, as follows:

- *Goals.* These are the statements of outcome. The session is designed around these goals; if you want to do an evaluation of each session, use them as your benchmarks.

- *Methodology.* This describes briefly what learning techniques you are employing. The methodology is not complicated and is already familiar to you if you have led a workshop or a class. The learning techniques employed are:

  Presentation. Didactic imparting of information. Used when you tell people facts that they are not expected to know. You can read the presentation word-for-word from your manual or rephrase it in your own words.

  Presentation and discussion. Some imparting of information, but this is information that some people in the group may be familiar with or that is similar enough to something familiar that the participants can help teach each other. The discussion helps keep people engaged, and this methodology is used where there is more than one right answer.

  Exercise. This general-purpose word describes any number of ways of getting the group or parts of the group to teach themselves something. Exercises are done with the whole group; in pairs, small groups, and report-backs from small groups; and working alone. In pairs or working alone, the report-back is voluntary, and not every pair or individual will speak to the whole group. Some exercises involve role play or practice, in which people take on roles they will encounter in reality and work with them to become comfortable with the process. Role play is used extensively in all aspects of asking for money on the phone or in person.

- *Time.* This is an approximation of how long it takes you to prepare for and present each session.

- *Notes.* These are suggestions about how to lead this particular session and materials you may need to prepare ahead of time.

- *Content.* This is the point at which the session begins; it demarcates the end of what you need to know to get ready for the session and the beginning of the description of what you actually do in the session.

- *Homework.* This has the same meaning as it did in school.

- *Wrap-up.* This brings the class to a close. Within the wrap-up there are usually two parts (often followed by a summary). *Key learnings* have participants take one or two minutes to write down what they most want to remember or what they most learned about themselves from the session just completed. There is no need for them to share the learnings; they are a way to get participants to note information or insights that are most useful to them personally. In *evaluation,* you ask participants to review the goals and tell you whether the session met those goals. This is not an evaluation of you as a leader, although you may receive constructive criticism or suggestions. It is more an evaluation of the pacing and content, and a chance for participants to take ownership of the class so that it is a true team effort. You may find after a few sessions that spending more than a minute on evaluation is not necessary, but it is a way to ensure that no problems fester. Finally in the wrap-up, you summarize what participants should have learned (you may want to refer to your goals) and tell them what they will learn next time. You can also restate any homework assignments or other commitments that have been made during the session.

LOGISTICS OF THE SESSION

You need a flipchart, easel, and dark-colored markers for every session. You can also work with a dry-erase board and markers. A blackboard will do, but it is not as helpful visually as paper or the dry-erase board because it is harder to read. Use only black or blue markers for words. Green or red can be used for highlights, but they are hard to read.

Ideally, participants sit around a table, so that they can refer to their manuals and take notes easily. School desks are also fine. Arrange the tables or desks in a U-shape, with you and the flipchart(s) at the front.

It is critical that sessions start and end on time, since much is included in each session. If from the very beginning you start the sessions on time, no matter how many people are attending they will come on time to subsequent meetings. In a one-hour session, there is no need to serve refreshments.

You will probably want to have a small podium or a table to spread out your notes and papers.

Always bring one or two extra copies of the participant's manual for those who have forgotten theirs. Also, bring paper and pens for people who don't come prepared to take notes.

DOING MORE THAN ONE SESSION AT A TIME

If you elect to do several sessions at one longer meeting, such as a weekend retreat or in several half-days, give people a ten-minute break after the first hour and every 90–120 minutes after that. Do not expect to do more than six sessions in a row. If you are doing this as a retreat, start with Session 1 the night the retreat begins (say, Friday). The next day, do the next four sessions in Part One, followed by a lunch break. Bring people back to begin Part Two, doing Sessions 6 through 8. The next day, you can finish the remaining six sessions in a row. It will be exhausting but exhilarating. You will probably want a co-trainer to help you.

You may also wish to complete Part One (fundraising basics) in the context of a daylong retreat, use six one-hour sessions to take participants through Part Two (choosing the appropriate strategy), and then end with a half-day or full-day retreat for Part Three (creating a fundraising plan).

SOME TIPS ON TRAINING

In a classroom setting, it is important to remember that the needs and desires of the whole group take priority over the needs or desires of an individual. It is helpful to start with some ground rules that establish this in a gentle way. Here are commonly accepted ground rules:

- *Allow no side conversations.* If someone has a question or a comment, let the group benefit from it. If someone wants to say something to another privately, ask the person to wait for a break.
- *Ask people to raise their hands and wait to be called on.* Unless you are working with a very small group (fewer than seven people), allowing people to speak without being recognized means that only people comfortable speaking in that way participate. The ideas and insights of members who are shyer will be lost. This is particularly important if you have people in your class for whom English is a second language, or if you have a variety of education or class backgrounds. A few well-educated, confident people can easily dominate a class. These sessions depend on all the participants' being able to speak up.
- *Vary the routine for generating discussion.* You can ask who wants to talk, you can go around the room and make everyone say something, or you can call on people who haven't spoken or who you think have something valuable to say.

- *Always validate what participants say.* Nod your head to encourage them, and if you think they made a good point, say so. If they say something that is not correct, either ask them why they think what they do or gently correct them. Often people have incorrect perceptions about fundraising that they have read or heard; before correcting them, you can say, "A lot of people think that," or "That is the most common perception, but. . . ."

- *Use the flipchart.* It is a good place to record answers to questions and then provide correct information by referring to what is written on the chart. Once something is written down, most people forget who said it; with this technique, the person who said it won't need to feel embarrassed if he or she made a mistake.

- *Encourage mistakes and uncertainty.* Remember that people learn more from mistakes than successes. If, as you prepare for these classes, you find some information surprising, or it contradicts what you previously thought, tell the group that. This gives them permission to ask questions or raise concerns.

- *Acknowledge your own mistakes.* Whether or not you are a professional trainer or group leader, if you make a mistake acknowledge it and start over. The people in the group are your friends and colleagues, and they will help you out.

- *Use your materials.* You may want to use notes or mark your manual so that you can refer to it easily, but try not to be tied to your notes. Look up every few seconds and make sure the group is engaged. When you ask if there are questions, look at the group and count to ten silently before proceeding. This reassures everyone that you want to hear their questions.

Above all, keep it light and have fun teaching this material. Raising the money we need for our cause is serious business; paradoxically, this is why we can't take ourselves or our teaching that seriously. Almost all religious traditions tell us that we are to have what we need. In the Christian tradition, Jesus says, "I came that you might have life and have it more abundantly." The Jewish tradition tells us that God desires "mercy and not sacrifice" and has simple requirements for us: "Do justice, love mercy, and walk humbly with God." A common Buddhist meditation blesses us with the phrase, "May all beings be happy." The Koran says that the person "who emigrates in God's way will find in the earth many resting-places and abundance . . . for God is forgiving and merciful."

As you prepare to teach this course, you may want to begin with a meditation for yourself. (You will note another one for participants in their manual.) I say this one to myself when I start a session: *"May the words of my mouth and the meditation of my heart be acceptable in Thy sight, my God, my rock, and my redeemer."*

Fundraising Basics

IN EVERYTHING WE TEACH, we make some basic assumptions about what people already know in order to proceed into what they don't know. In teaching cooking, we assume people know how many cups are in a quart, how to sift flour, and how to set the table; in preparing a worship service, we assume that the congregation knows how the hymnbook is numbered and what a responsive reading is. In leading people through something new to them, the tricky part is how to teach enough so that people are not confused and discouraged, but not to tell them so much that they feel bored or, worse, patronized.

The first section of this manual goes through the basics of fundraising. These are things that people must know to raise money effectively and that they tend not to know, or know only in part. Although some of this material is familiar to some people, probably no one in your group knows all of it; those who have some experience can be called on to share that experience. Avoid the temptation to skip over these building blocks; without this infrastructure, your fundraising program will draw up short later on.

As the leader, you may feel nervous that you are not familiar with this material. Try to put your nervousness aside and concentrate on preparing for the sessions. The material is not difficult to learn, and you may find that some of it is familiar. Recall when you had to master something unfamiliar and then teach it to someone else, and what made it possible for you to do that. Was it practicing ahead of time? Making your own notes? Rehearsing in front of the mirror? Tying an elaborate knot, learning to float, changing a tire, following a recipe, and balancing a checkbook are all examples of things you have probably learned and may have had to teach someone else.

Also, remember that in this first session, people may not be as forthcoming as they will be in later ones. Don't worry if silence meets your requests for response in this session, or if only a few people talk. As the sessions progress (or, if you are doing several sessions in one day, as the day progresses), people become more comfortable with each other and the discussions are easier.

SESSION 1 ✳ ✳ ✳ ✳ ✳ ✳ ✳ ✳ ✳ ✳

Who Gives, and Why?

OVERVIEW OF SESSION

Goals At the end of this session, participants will:

1. Know who gives away money and how much is available

2. Appreciate their own experience as givers and be able to apply that experience to thinking about raising money

3. Be familiar with one another's skills and experience with fundraising

Methodology Presentation and discussion

Time Thirty minutes to prepare, one hour to present

Notes
- If people want more information than is presented here, they can refer to the further readings in the Bibliography.

- This is a straightforward section, and little discussion is required.

- You can modify the opening exercise according to how well the participants already know each other, and how many participants there are.

SESSION 1

Content

BEGIN BY WELCOMING everyone to the first session of this fundraising course. Then proceed with a blessing, prayer, or meditation if you wish.

Take a few minutes to review the overall agenda of the course, pass out the participant's workbook, and review how the course is taught. ("We will meet here every Wednesday evening from 7:30 to 8:30. We will have food starting at 7:00, but the course will begin promptly at 7:30." Or "We will meet here after the worship service every Sunday for the next five weeks; then we will go on a daylong retreat to complete the course and make our own fundraising plan. That retreat is scheduled for April 13.")

Emphasize that it is important for people to be on time and to come to as many sessions as they possibly can. Review any other logistics (phone, bathrooms, availability of coffee or tea) that make people feel more comfortable. See if they have any questions or concerns about the overall course, and answer them as best you can.

When everyone is settled, begin with the opening exercise.

Introduction   (15 Minutes)

Introduce yourself and give a short description of why you are teaching this course and your experience with fundraising, including some of your experiences with giving away money. If you keep your introduction brief, the participants will follow your example. The amount of time per introduction depends on the number of people, but don't allow more than one minute each. For example:

> *My name is Alice Stein, and as you know, I'm the chair of the board of Jews Working for Peace. I've agreed to facilitate this course on fundraising because we're going to need a lot more money than we've raised in the past to ensure a strong Jewish voice for peace in the Middle East. My experience with fundraising includes putting on events, especially house parties, and asking friends for specific projects. I've written one fundraising letter and participated in the phone-a-thon at my temple. I also give away 10 percent of my income, so I know how I like to be asked and how I like to be treated as a donor. I'm really happy that all of us have made this commitment to learn fundraising.*

Ask all the participants to introduce themselves and give a brief description of their experience with fundraising.

Note how many people include the fact that they give money—whether it is a dollar to the collection plate or thousands to any nonprofit—as part of their experience with fundraising. Remind people that their experience as givers helps them become good askers.

Who Gives?   (Presentation; 10 Minutes)

Please note that you may add your own experience or additional information here, but don't leave anything out. Refer participants to page 9 in their workbooks.

> There are two sources of money for all the nonprofits in the United States: the public sector, which is the government, and the private sector. Government giving is financed primarily by taxes. Religious groups rarely receive government money. Groups like ours are financed almost entirely by the private sector.
> The private sector includes four sources of funding:
> 1. Living individuals
> 2. Bequests
> 3. Foundations
> 4. Corporations

Ask people to guess where they think most contributions come from. Write the correct information (given below) on the flipchart or blackboard as you talk. If you yourself were surprised when you read the information here, share your surprise with the group.

> Although it is hard to track exactly how much money is given by any of these sources, researchers working over the past fifty years have developed fairly accurate models to estimate how much money is given, by whom, and to what, based on tax returns, surveys, and published reports. They have reached these conclusions:
>
> - Living individuals give away 80-85 percent of all the money donated by the private sector.
> - Bequests, which are gifts made by living individuals through wills such that the receipt of the gift is deferred until the death of the donor, account for 5-7 percent of all private sector giving.
> - Corporations give 4-6 percent.
> - Foundations give 5-10 percent. (Remember also that the source of foundation money is almost always a bequest from an individual.)

Almost half of all the money given away by the private sector goes to religious institutions. Of course, the bulk of money religious institutions receive is given by individuals, which makes knowing how to raise money from individuals even more imperative for our work.

Ask if people are surprised by these figures, and why.

Remind them that if they get all their information about giving from the newspaper, they will be reading about extraordinary gifts from very wealthy donors. However, the truth about philanthropy is that ordinary people make it possible.

Would it surprise you to know that 82 percent of all the money given away by individuals comes from families with incomes of $60,000 or less? In fact, a 1994 study showed that families living on incomes of $10,000 gave away an average of 4.6 percent of their gross income, compared to an average of 1.1 percent of families living on incomes of $100,000. The middle class, working class, and poor are the ones giving the bulk of money in the private sector. Almost half of that money goes to religion, and about half of all the 1.1 million registered nonprofits in the United States are religious, so religious groups get exactly their market share of the money given away.

Why Do People Give?   (Discussion; 10 minutes)

First, give participants two or three minutes to reflect on their own giving, by listing in their workbooks two or three organizations they give to and why (page 10). Now, ask participants to reflect on why the people who have the least would be responsible for giving the most. Their answers might include:

- They are closer to the need.
- They are not as focused on making money.
- The majority of people are middle class, working class, or poor.

The third answer is the most accurate and is the one you should focus on.

The point is that the largest number of people give away the most money. Although many wealthy people are very generous, their giving does not make up the majority of giving. Foundations and corporations can be generous, but they are not responsible for giving most of the money. This is good news for us because it means that we already have access to all the people we must know to raise all the money we need. We are going to ask our friends and acquaintances, and when we have asked all of them, we will ask them who they know and begin to ask friends of friends. Remember also that people in lower income brackets sometimes do make very large gifts. For example, if someone earns $35,000 a year and believes in giving away 10 percent of her income, her total giving would be $3,500. The phrase *lower-income donor* does not mean we are going to get only small gifts from them, just as approaching *high-income donors* does not guarantee getting big gifts.

Questions for Further Discussion   (15 Minutes)

1. What would happen to our society if middle-class, working-class, and poor people realized that they are the ones who give away the most money?

2. In what ways does it help or hurt your ability to raise money to know that most of the people you ask can be people you know well?

3. How does naming yourself a "philanthropist" make you feel?

4. What is the difference between raising money for a religious project and a secular project?

Wrap-up

Ask participants to evaluate the session for five minutes. Start with what the key learnings are.

Key Learnings

1. _____

2. _____

3. _____

Use the short essay in Exhibit 1.1 as optional homework reading to spark further discussion or as a transition to the next session.

Introduce the next session: In the next session, we explore our personal attitudes toward money, and how they help and hurt us in our fundraising efforts.

Evaluation

Did the session meet its goals?

If there are things that need to be changed, make a note of them for next time. Also keep track of what people like so you can keep doing that.

If participants want changes, try to involve them in making the changes. For example, if they feel that the session sometimes goes too fast or too slow, ask them to share those feelings during the session, so it can be slowed down or speeded up. There will probably be few suggestions after the first session, but if you evaluate each session briefly and are open to making appropriate changes, the participants have a healthy sense of ownership of this course and can be most helpful to you.

EXHIBIT 1.1

Essay: Reclaiming Philanthropy

by Kim Klein

The Minnesota Council on Foundations has a delightful video called "What Is Philanthropy?" The filmmaker asks people on the street, "What is philanthropy?" "The study of monkeys," says one person. "Stamp collecting," says another. But for those people a little closer to the true definition, the answer is often, "When rich people give away money." However, because families living on incomes of $10,000 give away 4.6 percent of their income and families living on incomes of $100,000 give away 1.1 percent, I think it is fair to claim that our poorest community members are our most philanthropic, and that we have ceded the word *philanthropy* and the glory that comes with it to the extremely wealthy.

As all social activists know, a critical part of claiming power is claiming the right to name ourselves. For me, coming of age during the Women's Movement, it was important to say, "I am a woman, I am not a girl," and to be clear that the word *mankind* did not include me despite claims to the contrary. *People with disabilities* has taken the place of *handicapped* or *disabled* as a more accurate reflection of what having a disability means. We see similar patterns in terminology related to race and sexual orientation.

The word *philanthropist* comes from two words that mean "love of people." At its heart, that is what philanthropy is about. Understanding that anyone who values giving away money is a philanthropist allows people to see themselves as agents of change. "I have some money to give" is very different from the much more common refrain, "I don't know anyone with money," or "I don't have any money."

We all can give something. When put together with enough other people, that amount of money may be enough to do the work we think must be done.

Source: Adapted from the Grassroots Fundraising Journal *(vol. 18, no. 2, p. 3); reprinted with permission.*

SESSION 2 ✳ ✳ ✳ ✳ ✳ ✳ ✳ ✳ ✳ ✳

What Do You Think About Money?

OVERVIEW OF SESSION

Goals

At the end of this session, participants will:

1. Be able to identify the taboos and mysteries that surround the topic of money

2. Be able to specify what a healthy attitude toward money might be

3. Understand what our religious tradition teaches us about money

4. Be able to ask friends and colleagues for financial support for their organization

Methodology

Brainstorm, discussion and sharing, work alone, feedback to the whole group

Time

Thirty minutes to prepare, 75 minutes to present

SESSION 2

Content

WELCOME EVERYONE to the second session of the fundraising course. Then ask if there are questions or comments left over from the first session.

See if there are any comments or responses to the essay that ended Session 1. If there are new people, introduce them; you may also want to briefly review the agenda and schedule of the whole course. Make sure people have their workbooks. As soon as everyone is ready, introduce this session:

> Today, we're going to explore some of our learned attitudes toward money. We're hoping that in the end we will find attitudes and beliefs that help us reach our goal of being able to ask for money for our important work from friends, relatives, and colleagues.

Attitudes Toward Money   (Three Parts, 25 Minutes Total)

Our Attitudes   (Presentation)

> People are not born with opinions about money. In this exercise, we look at what our parents, the adults around us, our school, and our house of worship each taught us about money.
>
> Form pairs, and each person take two minutes to write in your workbook thoughts on questions 1 and 2. Then, tell your partner what you remember learning about money as a child or teenager. Your memories may include:
>
> - Old sayings, such as "Money doesn't grow on trees"
> - Perceptions that you had, although they may never have been voiced
> - Things you didn't believe then or that you don't agree with now
>
> You may have memories that are very different from those of your partner.

At the end of two minutes, ask participants to start sharing; after two more minutes, ask them to switch speakers.

Themes   (Discussion)

Bring the entire group back together and ask people to share the key points they remember; as they do, record them on your flipchart or blackboard. Your list probably includes:

- Don't ask people what their salary is.
- Money doesn't grow on trees.
- Money is the root of all evil.
- Don't ask anyone for money.
- Money talks.
- The "Golden Rule": who has the gold rules.
- Money is private.
- Money doesn't buy happiness.
- You can't take it with you.
- Don't buy on credit.
- Neither a borrower nor a lender be.
- People fight about money.

Ask the group to look at the list and notice the themes: negativity, privacy, power, and mixed messages. Note how some of the perceptions are false, such as the adage that "money is the root of all evil." Paul's letter to the Philippians says, "*The love of* money is the root of all evil."

A Healthy Attitude   *(Brainstorm)*

Now ask the group to think about what a healthy attitude toward money might look like, using the questions below. Make sure the whole group is engaged, so that this does not become a discussion among two or three people. Write responses to the questions on the flipchart.

- In an ideal world, what would people be taught as children to think about money?
- How would this change how we feel about money as adults?
- What does our religious tradition teach us about money?

Compare this list to the previous list. There are no right or wrong answers to any of the questions, but participants can see that what a healthy attitude might include and what they learned as children are probably very different. People may also discover that their scriptures actually have a very healthy view of the role of money. For example, in the Christian testament, Jesus talks five times as much about money and possessions as he does about prayer. The book of Exodus in the Torah describes a good society this way: "Those who had much did not have too much and those who had little did not have too little." All religious traditions emphasize that people are to trust in the goodness of God; they tell us that money is a tool.

Religious teaching focuses on behavior around money—how much to give away, whether to charge interest on a loan, the proper care of people who can't take care of themselves. It is wrong to steal, to be greedy, to make money more important than people. But no tradition teaches that money itself is evil or corrupting. Money can be used well, and it can be used badly. It can be solicited honestly or dishonestly. Money is simply a tool.

Allow this discussion to go on as long as the whole group seems engaged, and new information or insights are emerging. Emphasize that people do not need to agree on what a healthy relationship to money looks like, but they do need to acknowledge that the cultural norms about money are not that healthy.

Once you feel enough has been said on this topic, direct the participants' focus to the process of asking for a charitable donation. Point out that when we focus on asking for a gift to our cause, we face a cultural norm that asking for money is rude or scary, or that it can jeopardize a relationship.

Putting the Fear in Perspective　　(Optional Discussion; 5 Minutes)

If the religious project you are working on is controversial or out of the mainstream, this is a good time to help participants realize that by agreeing to be part of this project, they have already risked rejection. For example, a woman working in an anti–death penalty organization realized that by talking about the death penalty she was already being rude, according to cultural standards, because she was talking about death and politics, two other taboos. A man active in a Catholic church that has called for the ordination of women realized that he had already taken a scary step in asking that women be treated as equal to men. Helping participants realize that they have probably already said and done things far scarier and riskier than asking for money helps them let go of their anxiety about asking. Direct them to questions 3 and 4 in their workbooks and ask them to take two minutes to think about and jot down their thoughts.

Asking for Money　　　　　　　　　　(Brainstorm; 25 Minutes)

Have the participants imagine asking someone they know and respect for a relatively large amount of money (anything over $100). Ask them to jot in their workbooks (page 12) what they fear most about asking. This includes not only what the prospect might say or do, but also what the prospect might think of her and what she will think of herself.

Going around the group, have each participant say out loud one thing she is most afraid might be the outcome of her solicitation.

Write down all the feared outcomes on the flipchart. After four or five minutes, you will have a list that probably includes:

- The prospect will say no.
- The prospect will yell at me (or hit me).
- The prospect will give me the money but won't really want to and will resent me.
- I know the prospect doesn't have the money.
- It is imposing on our friendship for me to ask, and we won't be friends anymore.
- The prospect will think that the only reason I was nice to her was to get money.
- The prospect will say yes and then ask me for money for his cause.
- I don't know if my group really deserves the money as much as some other groups might.
- The prospect will ask me questions about the organization that I can't answer.

After this brainstorming session, ask the group to look at the fears and find common themes. They should notice that the fears fall into three categories:

1. Fear of things that will definitely happen some of the time (the person will say no)

2. Fear of things that may happen but can be dealt with if they do (the person will ask me for money; the person will ask questions I can't answer)

3. Fear of things that are extremely unlikely to happen (I'll be punched, I'll be sued, I'll throw up)

Lead the group through their list. For each fear, ask them to reflect on these questions:

- What are the chances that this will actually happen?
- If it happens, how much does it matter?
- What is the worst thing that can happen?

Concluding Comments for Asking for Money   (5 Minutes)

Looking at our fears makes them less scary and allows us to prepare ourselves properly for what might actually happen when we ask. For most people, the worst thing that can happen in asking for money is that the person will say no. But everyone who does fundraising is told no almost as often as they get a yes. Remember, just as it's your privilege to ask for money, it's the other person's privilege to turn you down. The person being asked may have just spent $1,000 on a car repair, or been solicited to give to five other organizations, or have other priorities. Sometimes people say no because they have other worries on their mind and can't take the time to think about your request. Perhaps they trust your friendship enough that they feel they can say no to you with no hard feelings. Although no one likes to be turned down, it's important not to take it as a personal rejection, because it almost never has anything to do with you.

The fear that someone will give to your organization and then ask you for money for his or her special cause requires remembering that if someone gives to your cause, you don't personally owe him a favor. The organization the check was made out to must now write him a thank-you note and do the work you said the group would do. The obligation to the donor (to the extent that it exists) is paid.

Fundraising is about an exchange: donors provide money in exchange for work being done that the donor believes in and wants to see happen. If the person you ask then asks you for his cause, you should think about whether it's a cause you believe in. If it is and you have the money, make the gift. If not, then don't. If you believe that a person's main motive for giving money is to be able to ask for money, exclude that person from your prospect list. You want to create a base of donors who are loyal to the organization, not to you, and especially not to any idea that he can now raise money from you.

Respond to questions you can't answer with "I don't know," or "I'll find out and let you know."

Fears such as "I know the person doesn't have the money" are very common. However, unless you have a financial statement from the person you are asking, or unless you know he or she is on welfare or has recently experienced a devastating financial setback, and so on, you *don't know* that the person doesn't have the money. Although most of us have had times when our financial situation was bleak, the fact is that how much money we feel we can give depends mostly on what mood we're in at the time we're asked and less on objective reality. Some days people feel generous, and some days they don't.

Sometimes it's not appropriate to ask someone for money, but this is true far less often than we think. If you consider asking someone for money and decide not to, ask yourself, "Do I have a *reason* not to ask, or just an *excuse* based on assumptions I'm making about the other person?"

Now that we've looked at our fears about asking, we're ready to examine what it's like to be the person giving the money. This is much more familiar territory for all of us, since we've all given away money.

Being Asked for Money   (Discussion; 10 Minutes)

Ask participants to imagine that an acquaintance—someone they like and respect but don't know well—has come to them, explained a cause he or she is involved in, and asked for a gift. The participants should imagine that the gift is an affordable amount but not one they could give without some thought. For most people, this amount is somewhere between $50 and $250.

Give the participants thirty seconds to write in their workbooks (page 12) all the reasons they would say yes to this request. Then give them thirty seconds to list all the reasons they would say no.

On the flipchart or blackboard, create two columns, labeled "Yes" and "No." Ask participants to share their lists, and record them in the appropriate column. There are generally more yes reasons than no reasons. Here are the most common reasons:

Why I Would Say Yes

Like the person asking

Believe in the cause

Get something for my money

Tax deduction

Feeling generous

Just got paid

Know my money will be well used

Want to support my friend

Feel guilty saying no

Know other people in the group

Don't have time to volunteer, so give money

Liked the approach

Why I Would Say No

Don't believe in the cause

Don't have the money

Bad mood that day

Organization has a bad reputation

Give to other things

Already been asked several times that week

Don't know what my money will be used for

Think person asking is naïve or pushy

Ask the group to discuss the two lists. Again, let the conversation range freely. After five minutes, from what people have listed draw from the group the conclusions discussed next.

On the no list, the reasons fall into two categories. The first is that it's not the asker's fault, and this couldn't be known ahead of time. The asker usually cannot know that the prospect doesn't have the money right now, or that he's in a bad mood, or has been asked several times that week. If this is the reason for the rejection, you can only thank the prospect for his time and go on to the next prospect.

Second, the answer appears to be no but is really "maybe." If the prospect (1) knew more about the organization, (2) knew how the money was to be used, or (3) knew whether the reasons for the organization's bad reputation have been cleared up, he or she might give. These no answers are really maybe ("Maybe I'd give if I thought the organization did good work"; "Maybe I'd give if I were in a better mood"; "Maybe I'd give if you'd been the first group to ask me instead of the sixth").

You may be able to discuss the prospect's reasons for saying no and either change the answer to an affirmative or learn something useful that helps in the next solicitation.

A few of the no reasons may reflect badly on you as the asker. For example, if the prospect thinks you are naïve or pushy or if he dislikes you altogether, then this is an unfortunate choice of person for a solicitation.

Wrap-up

Repeat the lessons that the group has learned through the exercises they have done. You may ask the group to draw final conclusions, or you may wish to end the session with a short lecture based on two points:

1. The exercises and the subsequent discussion have helped you understand that asking for money is not as frightening as you may have thought.

2. The worst thing that can happen is that the person asked will say no; usually she says no for reasons outside your control or knowledge.

Here is a suggestion for a short lecture, if you prefer it:

You have to keep in mind why you're asking for money. *What you believe in needs to be bigger than what you're afraid of.* We need to be very clear about what we believe, why we believe it, and what we're willing to do for our beliefs. Being turned down on a request for money is a relatively minor sacrifice.

Now, introduce the next session:

The next session helps us understand what an organization must have in place before it's ready to raise money, and helps us create our "case statement."

Key Learnings

1. _____
2. _____
3. _____

Evaluation

Did this session meet its goals?

What You Need Before You Begin Raising Money

OVERVIEW OF SESSION

Goals At the end of this session, participants will:

1. Understand that fundraising is a process of exchange
2. Know the most important elements in asking for money
3. Understand the purpose and elements of a case statement
4. Be able to articulate clearly the mission of their organization

Methodology Introductory comments, discussion, brainstorm, work in teams, work alone

Time Thirty minutes to prepare; one hour to present plus homework

Note
- In addition to reviewing the materials carefully, read the outline of the case statement provided in the participant's workbook.

- In this segment, be sure to take into account that you should encourage a lot of discussion and commentary all the way through, and allow for that in keeping track of time.

- If the group already has a case statement or materials that can fairly easily be converted to a case statement, then work with those materials and revise this session to help participants decide if the case statement they are working with is adequate or needs any improvement.

- Whether you work with an existing statement or create part of a new one, participants still need to go through the exercises to help them identify the most exciting aspects of their group and how they might present them.

SESSION 3

Content

WELCOME EVERYONE to this session. Then ask if there are any questions or comments left over from the last session. If there are new people, or if someone missed the last session, ask participants for a two-minute summary of the key learnings from that session. Once everyone is settled, introduce this session.

The Exchange Principle   (Presentation; 2 minutes)

Fundraising is about exchange: a donor gives money to an organization in exchange for that group doing work that the donor thinks is important. Sometimes the exchange is fairly direct: a donor gives money to help buy a new organ for the sanctuary, and his reward is better music when he comes to church. More often, the exchange is not so direct: a donor gives money to an Tibetan aid group so that Tibetan refugee children living in India can go to school. She can see pictures of them and their school, but their lives don't directly affect hers.

Sometimes the exchange can't be measured easily: a donor gives money so that members of his synagogue can attend a conference on how the religious community can address Third World debt. Whatever the exchange, it's important to realize that fundraising is not begging. Begging is when you ask for something you have literally done nothing to deserve. If a project or an organization deserves money, then it's not begging if it asks for money. When an organization seeks donations, there is an implicit contract with the donors: pay us to do work that you want to see done.

In this session, we create a statement about what work we are doing that will be exchanged for donations. In this process, we get to experience the importance of being straightforward in putting forth what we want.

What Makes a Successful Request   (Exercise; 20 minutes)

This exercise helps participants reflect on what distinguishes a successful request from one that is not so successful.

Ask five participants to act out the scenario described on page 15 of the Participant Manual. One person plays himself or herself as the listener, and the other four play the four neighbors, each with their own approach. The participants should read the scenario and then take one minute to act out each approach. The following instructions appear in the participant's workbook.

> *Situation: Your neighbor's car cannot be driven and he or she needs groceries. Here are four ways the neighbor tells you about his or her need:*
>
> *Neighbor one's approach: "My car is broken and there's no food in the house. I don't know what to do."*
>
> *Neighbor two's approach: "My car is broken and I need groceries. I was wondering if I could borrow your car for an hour to go to the store."*
>
> *Neighbor three's approach: "Are you going to the grocery store anytime soon? My car is broken and I need some food, so I was hoping to hitch a ride with you."*
>
> *Neighbor four's approach: "My car is broken and you have two cars, so could you lend me one for a while?"*

Ask participants to discuss these questions:

- Which approach is most effective, and why?

- How would you like to be approached in this situation?

- How can we apply what we learn from these approaches to asking for money?

Most participants see that the straightforward approaches of neighbors two and three are most effective. Participants may disagree on whether the first approach or the last one is more offensive, but you should point out that passive hinting or demanding out of a sense of entitlement are both ineffective ways to ask for a favor.

Elements of Making or
Receiving a Request   (Discussion; 10 Minutes)

Use these supposition and discussion questions:

> Think about the last time you asked someone for something that they were not obligated to give you or do for you.

- Was it difficult to ask?
- Did you prepare for making the request?
- Did you try to anticipate what the person would say?

What do you want to know from someone who asks you for something?

Ask participants to notice the similarities and differences between how they like to be approached for a favor and how they prepare themselves to ask someone else for a favor.

The responses to both questions tend to be similar and often include the elements needed in either making or receiving a request:

- A reason

- A time frame

- Clarity about exactly what you want

- Graciousness in receiving a request

- Willingness to be turned down or to turn down

Next, have people reflect on how they feel when they need to say no to someone. People can simply reflect on the question or use the scenario of the car request, with the assumption that they have a policy of not lending their car. In either case, participants should discuss these points:

- Is it hard to say no?

- How do you feel about being asked for something when you have to say no?

- What makes saying no easier?

- How does understanding the exchange principle help here?

Conclusion to Successful Request   (Presentation; 5 Minutes)

If we reflect on our own experiences of asking and giving, and if we look at hypothetical scenarios, we notice some things we've known all along: when asking, be straightforward about what you want and when you want it, and be gracious with whatever the response is. In terms of fundraising, this means knowing that your organization deserves support and is not begging when it solicits donations; even so, the person you are asking is not obligated to help you.

Ask participants to reflect on the exchange principle in their religious tradition, and to reflect on how their religious understanding of exchange might help in their fundraising.

For example, a young Buddhist said, "My meditation has allowed me to feel free from the need to control other people, because I can't. I can't even control what's going to happen to me in the next five minutes. Among other things, this insight enables me to be an excellent fundraiser. I present the cause and ask for the money. I'm grateful for whatever response I get."

A Catholic nun working as a doctor in Nicaragua says, "God says, 'I have come that you might have life and have it more abundantly.' Certainly, that's my experience and what I try to give back in my work. When I raise money for my ministry, I find the same desire in the donors—to take their abundance and share it. It has become a pleasure to ask for money because it gives people so much pleasure to give it."

Once participants understand the exchange principle, they must think through exactly what their organization is exchanging. This is called the preparation of the case. To be effective stewards of money, we must know why we are raising money, what we intend to spend it on, and how we are going to evaluate our work. If we do not have a clear case, we may wind up squandering resources that have been shared with us.

Case Statement   (Presentation; 15 Minutes)

Our task is to create a document that provides all the information we need when we ask for money.

This document is called a *case statement.* It describes in detail the need an organization was set up to meet, how the organization will meet that need, and the capacity of the organization to meet that need.

It's an internal document, used by staff, board, volunteers— people close to the organization. It is not a secret document, but it's generally too long and cumbersome to copy and circulate widely.

Parts of it are used in brochures, proposals, direct mail appeals, and the like, and nothing that's written or said by anyone in the group contradicts anything in the case statement.

Have participants find the elements of the case statement in their workbooks (beginning on page 16) and follow along as you review it with them. Take them through all the parts of it without examples first, so that they are familiar with the words. After this review, you will work through each part using examples. You may find it useful to write the key words on the flipchart as you go along.

Elements of the Case Statement

- *Mission* (the "why"). Why does this group exist, or why is this project being created? The mission statement consists of one or two sentences that tell a little about the group; it is a statement of passion and belief. It expresses the basic premise of the group.

- *Goals* (the "what"). What does the organization intend to accomplish over the long run? In other words, what does the organization intend to do about why it exists?

- *Objectives* (the "how"). Objectives are statements that give specific, measurable, and realistic outcomes describing exactly how the goals will be met in a specific time frame (usually one year).

- *History.* This is a short narrative that shows the organization is competent and can accomplish its goals. If there is no organizational history, as in the case of a new project, summarize the qualifications of the people putting the project together.

- *Structure.* This short narrative describes who is involved in the group and the roles of volunteers, board members, and staff; it shows that you have the right people involved and they have appropriate roles in implementing the work of the group.

- *Budget.* The budget is a projection of income and expenses for the current year and a financial statement for the previous fiscal year to demonstrate that you are spending the right amount of money and getting it from the right sources.

Creating the Case Statement   During the rest of this session and in Session 4, you will take participants through each section of the case statement and have them begin working on the actual language for their group. In this session, they work out the mission statement. In Session 4, they work out goals and construct the rest of the case.

A mission statement answers the question *why*. Answers to such a question almost always begin with "Because . . ." or "We believe. . . ." To create effective mission statements, do not begin with "To. . . ." *To feed, to clothe, to house, to teach, to heal*—these are goals. If you want to create a mission state-

Point out to participants that mission statements can differ in length but should not be too long. They can state a belief or summarize a solution to a problem, but they name something basic about the work of the group, so that the hearer knows what belief the goals and the objectives of the group arise from.

If all the participants are from the same organization, take ten minutes to see if you can agree on the wording of a mission statement, or at least the beginning words of a mission statement. Make an agreement about how the final mission statement will be written.

Questions for Reflection   (Optional; 10 Minutes)

- What is the mission statement of our faith tradition?
- What is the mission statement of the United States?
- What is your personal mission statement?

Homework

Ask participants to recall the history of their organization, especially in terms of accomplishments. Knowing what the group has been able to do and not do ensures that future plans are realistic.

Wrap-up

Getting an accurate mission statement is perhaps the most difficult part of developing the case statement. The other parts of the case—and of the organization's work—flow from this mission statement. In the next session, we work on creating the other elements of the case statement.

Key Learnings

1. _____

2. _____

3. _____

Evaluation

Did the session meet its goals?

SESSION 4 ✳ ✳ ✳ ✳ ✳ ✳ ✳ ✳ ✳ ✳

Completing the Case Statement

OVERVIEW OF SESSION

Goals At the end of this session, participants will:

1. Understand how the parts of the case statement go together

2. Have experience working on the remaining elements of the case statement

3. Understand the importance of having a clear case statement before proceeding to raise money

Methodology Presentation, discussion, brainstorm, work in teams, work alone

Time Thirty minutes to prepare; 60–90 minutes to present (depending on degree of discussion needed)

Note • Before the session, obtain a copy of the budget of the organization. If people in the training are from more than one organization, obtain a copy of the budget for the organization most people are from. Make enough copies of this budget to hand out at the end of the session.

SESSION 4

Content

WELCOME EVERYONE to this session. Then ask if there are any questions or comments left over from the last session. If someone missed the last session, ask participants for a two-minute summary of the key learnings from that session.

If you were able to achieve any agreement about your mission statement, start with that. Otherwise, review the process for deciding on the final wording of a mission statement. As soon as everyone is settled, begin with the opening exercise.

Goals

Help and Hindrance   *(Pairs; 5-7 Minutes)*

Ask the group to form pairs and for each person to take a minute to think back silently to any clear goal they ever committed themselves to that was going to take a long time to accomplish. Examples might be going to college, saving money to buy a house or go on a big trip, or training for a marathon. After a minute, ask each person to share his or her reflections with the partner, keeping in mind these questions:

- How did having a long-term goal help you work on your goal weekly or monthly?
- Did having a goal hinder you in any way?

After five minutes, bring the group back together. Ask people to share some of the highlights of their comments, and capture them on the flipchart in two columns, with the headings shown here. Comments may include:

How a Goal Helped Me	*How a Goal Hindered Me*
Gave me a clear focus for my energy	Sometimes became obsessed with the goal and forgot to live my life
Made it easy to figure out objectives and tasks	Sometimes forgot that other people have their own goals
Was motivating; even when bogged down in detail, I remembered the goal and kept going	Having set goal, was hard to see any other way to get what I wanted except by reaching it
Gave me a reason to work hard	
Made me feel good about myself	

Now ask the group to reflect on how having goals for an organization is helpful, and in what ways might they be hindering.

The purpose of this discussion is to remind the group that goals are very important, if they are kept in perspective. Goals give direction and point to the mission—they are not in themselves the direction or the end point.

Mission-derived Goals   (Brainstorm and Discussion; 10 Minutes)

Using the flipchart, write up your mission statement, or whatever sentences are the closest to your final mission statement. If there are people from more than one organization in the room, use the mission statement from the group that most people are from.

Then ask the group to give you goals that would go with that mission statement. Explain that goals are statements that begin with "To. . . ." Goals are broad, general statements that tell what the organization is going to do to act on the belief it has put forward in its mission statement.

Refer participants to the goals for the three organizations whose mission statements were given in Session 3. (These goals are reproduced in the Participant Manual, pages 20–21.)

1. The ecumenical housing coalition. The mission statement:

   We believe housing should be a right, not a privilege.

Possible goals:

- To ensure that all major Protestant and Catholic churches in our community see providing permanent housing for poor families as a ministry of their church

- To offer financing so that poor families can buy homes and begin to build financial security

- To help families with no credit or poor credit create a positive credit history

- To assist families in budgeting, job seeking, child care, and other needs

- To serve as a witness to the government and to other faith traditions of the pressing need for a solution to our city's ongoing housing crisis

2. The domestic violence program. The mission statement:

   We believe that violence is never an appropriate response to a domestic conflict.

Possible goals:

- To be a clear voice that the Jewish community does not condone domestic violence

- To teach conflict-resolution techniques so that children and adults no longer respond to stressful situations with physical or verbal violence
- To provide sanctuary for survivors of domestic violence while alternative housing is arranged
- To educate religious professionals, particularly clergy, about their role in preventing domestic violence

3. The interfaith peace organization. The mission statement:

   We believe that interfaith dialogue is essential for peace and racial and ethnic harmony.

Possible goals:

- To bring clergy together from a variety of traditions and help them introduce interfaith dialogue into their houses of worship
- To create and disseminate curricula reflecting an ecumenical viewpoint that can be used in Sunday schools, parochial schools, and other settings where children are learning about their own faith tradition
- To present a religious voice to the broadcast media that is open-minded and thoughtful rather than dogmatic

Be sure that participants understand that goals are realistic descriptions of outcomes, but with no time limit. A goal may take a lifetime to accomplish, but a goal is theoretically possible. Goals allow people to give specific words to their visions and force people to articulate exactly what the outcome of the mission of the organization would be. In social justice or social service work, goals imply that someday the group will not be needed because the goal will be accomplished.

Religious projects and organizations need to state their goals or else they will find that goals are stated for them—and the goals imputed to them are usually unattractive. For example, the domestic violence program in the synagogue was described in the newspaper as, "A program to help wives learn how not to provoke their husbands to violence." Because they had clear goals, they could quickly respond that they do not condone violence in the home at all, and they reject the sexist idea that violence against women is provoked by women.

The ecumenical housing coalition spent many hours deciding whether the families who were helped had to be members of a church. Their goals reflect their decision that they did not, which allowed them to easily deflect the accusation that they were promoting a religious agenda with the families they helped.

Once you are certain that participants understand the reason for having clear goals, you can move on to creating objectives.

Objectives (Presentation, Small Groups, Discussion; 15 Minutes)

Objectives name work that is specific and achievable in a certain time frame. For example:

- This year, four new churches will contribute $10,000 each to help make down payments available on four houses.
- This year our curricula on conflict resolution will be used in ten Protestant Sunday schools, reaching two hundred children ages eight to twelve.
- All synagogues in our community will participate in Domestic Violence Awareness Month.

Objectives don't spell out in detail the tasks required to accomplish the objective, but they do say what will happen, with whom, and by when. They answer the question, "How will you go about meeting your goals?"

There is an acronym that helps design objectives. It says that objectives are SMART:

- Specific
- Measurable
- Achievable
- Realistic
- Time-limited

Once you have a clear mission, goals, and objectives, you can illustrate what you mean with stories of your accomplishments. Stories make the case statement come alive and allow listeners to understand what you do from the point of view of people you affect. The stories are examples of why the goals are important, or of how the objectives will be accomplished.

Here are two sample stories from the groups whose mission and goals we've discussed. Note how the stories bring the work into focus and add the human element that makes listeners want to help. The first is from the ecumenical housing coalition, and the second from the domestic violence program:

• Mary Murphy and her mother, Anna, lived in a trailer park. Their trailer was cold in the winter, hot in the summer. Water leaked in around the windows, and the foundation was unsafe. Mary has a steady job as a janitor, and her mother has a small pension. They can afford monthly payments but do not have savings for a down payment or even a deposit on a rental. We provided the down payment for them on a two-bedroom bungalow near Mary's workplace. They are typical of America's working poor, and they just need a little help.

• Our work with clergy has resulted in ten houses of worship, from Protestant to Catholic to Jewish to Buddhist, agreeing to make domestic violence the subject of sermons, talks, or meditations during Domestic Violence Awareness Month. One Baptist minister told us that five women in his congregation—including the wife of the board chair—came to him after his sermon to talk about the violence in their homes.

What are some stories our group could tell?

Now it is time for participants to work on goals and objectives for their own group (page 21 in their workbooks).

Divide the participants into as many small groups as there are going to be goals, with no fewer than three people in each small group. If there are more goals than participants, then give each small group more than one goal to work on. Tell them each group is to come up with one to five objectives for each goal, and then report back to the group. After ten to fifteen minutes, bring the whole group back together and discuss some of the objectives from the small groups. Be sure to capture these on the flipchart.

Ask participants what they learned from this exercise. Answers will include:

• Hard to be specific.

• This is what planning is all about.

• This will help us get our work done.

The exercises in the next section, on history and budget, can be done during this session, or separately. This depends on how long you let the discussion continue on creating goals and objectives, and how involved and excited people are about the goals and objectives they have come up with for their group. If people are really engaged in discussion, do not force an end to the process, but let the decisions about what goals and objectives to adopt, continue with, or abandon go on to its natural conclusion. On the other hand, if people are floundering—or, ideally, if they have achieved consensus and are ready to move on—then proceed to the next exercise.

History   (Discussion; 15-20 Minutes)

Ask members of the group to recall the history of the organization. As they talk, create a time line on the flipchart. If there are other people in your congregation or community who would remember more about how the program started and what it has accomplished, then invite them to participate in the discussion. Explain to the participants that understanding and appreciating the history of the group helps give them the passion needed to raise money for it. Also, because objectives soon become history, this discussion helps further clarify the need for good, easy-to-understand objectives. Following the discussion, give participants three minutes to note in their workbooks three milestones related to their organization's mission (page 22).

It costs money to implement objectives, and the final part of the case preparation is the budget.

Budget   (Presentation and Discussion; 15-30 Minutes)

Ask a volunteer or staff person to present the budget and walk people through it. Make sure that everyone understands the income and expenses and agrees that the expenses are appropriate and sufficiently accounted for. Explain that by feeling confident in the budget, participants will be more eager to raise the money needed.

If your organization has not kept good records or has been sloppy in its budget-making and evaluating process, then this discussion will take more than fifteen minutes. Avoid engaging in accusations of mismanagement or carelessness, and by all means disallow gossiping about people who are not in the room, regardless of their role in whatever budget problems you may be having. The important thing to focus on is the two-part question, "What is our budget now, and how can we monitor and evaluate it?"

In budgeting, religious groups often get themselves into more trouble than their secular counterparts do. First, because they are often run by volunteers, it is hard to keep track of all expenses. Volunteers wind up paying for a lot of things out of pocket, and the group does not have a clear sense of how much it really costs to do business. Second, religious congregations (which some religious groups are not) have more lenient reporting requirements to the IRS and so do not have as much outside pressure to be exact.

There is a high level of trust among religious people, which is rarely violated but can lead to sloppy or nonexistent bookkeeping. Often a volunteer sets up a bookkeeping system and then passes it on to another volunteer. That person changes the system to one she understands, passes it on, and so forth . . . and after several changes, no one understands it.

Organizations do well to ask someone in a secular nonprofit to help them set up a simple bookkeeping system. Computer programs make this much easier than it used to be.

Participants need to make a decision about how they want to keep track of income and expenses, and how they want to create and monitor their budget. If they cannot make a decision about that in this session, establish a process and set a date by which a decision will be made.

Homework

Ask for two or three volunteers to compile all the work that has been done on the case statement and have copies to pass out at the next meeting.

Wrap-up

The case statement is the most important working document for fundraising, so you should feel free to take as much time as is required to create a good case statement and be sure it is approved by the board of directors as representing the organization well. The next session is on the critical role of volunteers in the fundraising process.

Key Learnings

1. _____

2. _____

3. _____

Evaluation

Did this session meet its goals?

SESSION 5 ✳ ✳ ✳ ✳ ✳ ✳ ✳ ✳ ✳ ✳

The Role of Volunteers in Fundraising

OVERVIEW OF SESSION

Goals
At the end of this session, participants will:

1. Understand that in a volunteer-run organization, all the volunteers must be part of the fundraising program in some way

2. See themselves as part of a fundraising team

3. Realize the importance of setting an example in fundraising

4. Be able to organize other volunteers to help with fundraising

Methodology
Discussion, reflective questions, small-group work, individual work

Time
Thirty minutes to prepare, one hour to present

Notes
• Since all or the majority of the people in the group are volunteers, this session focuses on how to get all of them to find a role in fundraising that feels comfortable. In addition to being volunteers, many in more than one capacity, most will also have recruited other volunteers. Therefore, this is a good opportunity to ask other participants to help you present the content of this session, or even present the whole session so that you can participate.

- If the group that is working together is part of a board of directors, or will be forming a board of directors, use the section on the role of the board to develop a coherent understanding of their roles. If the group is not going to be part of a board, skip that part and go to the presentation on building a volunteer team.

- Please note that, depending on your group, the presentation of the case statement and its ensuing discussion may take an extra session, or an extra hour or two. As the facilitator, you must exercise judgment on how long to let the discussion continue. You don't want to shortchange it, because the content of the case statement is the basis of all your planning and the expression of your vision. On the other hand, you don't want participants to be bogged down in semantics or allow one or two people to slow down the whole process. You may wish to confer with one or two other participants in deciding how to handle this.

SESSION 5

Content

WELCOME participants to this session. Review what happened in Session 4 for people who might have missed it. When everyone has settled down, begin with the homework from last session.

If the people compiling the case statement have completed that work, take fifteen to twenty minutes to review what they have done.

Homework Review   (15–20 Minutes)

- Ask what questions or confusions the compilers discovered as they put the case statement together. The groups should respond to those with either clarification or a decision about how clarification will be reached.

- Ask the group to tell the compilers of the statement if there are any confusions or questions they have based on what has been put together. (This will probably not be the final version of the case statement, but will need to go back to a small committee for further work. Make sure the work of that committee is clear, and set a deadline for completing this next round of work. Ideally, a workable case statement will be ready by the next session.)

- Ask if there are any further questions or comments on the idea of fundraising as an exchange and the case statement as the fundamental description of what the group is exchanging for donations. When you feel participants are finished with this discussion, begin with the opening exercise.

Personal Volunteer Experiences   (Exercise; 15 Minutes)

Ask participants to take two minutes to make notes to themselves in their workbooks (page 24) on the answers to the following questions:

- What was your first volunteer experience?

- What was your best volunteer experience?

- What was your worst volunteer experience?

Give each participant one minute to tell the group his or her answers to these questions. Ask someone to volunteer to keep time by holding up a hand after thirty seconds and by saying "Time" after one minute. At the end of the minute, the group moves to the next participant, whether the speaker is finished or not. There are no comments and no questions during the storytelling. As the leader, start with your own responses to the questions, setting an example of a one-minute description.

After everyone has spoken, ask participants to reflect on what made experiences good or bad, using the questions that follow to guide the discussion. Use the flipchart to record highlights of the observations.

- What influence did the first experience seem to have on the other two?

- What role did personalities play in the experiences?

- What role did the organization's being organized or disorganized play?

- What did you learn about yourself from these experiences?

- What would you advise someone new to volunteering to be aware of?

    Generally, the conclusions include these instances of best experience:

- Fun group of people

- Good leadership

- Specific project that I felt qualified to help with

- People patient with me

- Felt appreciated

and these of worst experience:

- All the work I had done was changed or thrown out.

- The leader of the project could not delegate.

- The leader of the project thought she knew everything.

- I was asked to do things I didn't know how to do, and then blamed for not doing them right.

- The work seemed never-ending.

Now give participants a minute or two to reflect on the additional questions about volunteering on page 25 in their workbook. Then bring the attention to focus on the times they volunteered to help with fundraising (some may have already spoken about this in their best and worst experiences). What made their fundraising experience good or bad? Note any similarities or differences from overall volunteer experience.

Similarities may include:

- Need for clear structure and time frame

- Importance of good leadership

- Sense of accomplishment and being appreciated

Differences may include:

- Fundraising is more anxiety-provoking than other kinds of volunteering.

- Few people want to help with fundraising.

- We spent a lot of time talking about what we were going to do before we were able to decide how to proceed.

Volunteering for Fundraising   (Presentation; 15 Minutes)

Fundraising is a task that few people really want to do, yet everyone agrees it must be done. Most organizations have observed that for fundraising to be effective, the work needs to be divided fairly among the whole group. If we look at what we know about how to make volunteer experiences good, we can use that knowledge in ensuring that people's experiences with fundraising are good and that they feel appreciated and willing to keep working on fundraising.

The organization must create a culture in which people realize that fundraising is a part of everyone's job. It's very similar to coming to and participating in meetings, being a good listener, helping with cleanup after an event, or the dozens of other tasks that work best when spread among a team.

People volunteer for religious projects for many of the same reasons they volunteer for anything, but also because they want to grow spiritually and work with like-minded people. Sometimes volunteers in religious organizations don't want to deal with money at all.

Ask participants what differences they have noted in how people in religious programs or projects deal with fundraising in contrast to secular projects.

Differences may include:

- Denial of the need to really raise money (believing that "God will provide" sometimes serves as a way to not be involved in fundraising)

- Feeling that money should come from the denomination or some source other than the fundraising efforts of volunteers

- Wishing to leave the world of money behind when taking on work for a religious project

- Fear of corrupting the personal spiritual journey with concerns about money

Engage participants in a short discussion about how to avoid any of these problems in the fundraising efforts your group is undertaking (ten minutes at most).

The Role of the Board   (Optional, Presentation, and Discussion; 20 Minutes)

> Board members are volunteers with very specific roles in the organization. The purpose of the board of directors is to run the organization effectively and to act as its "legal guardians." To qualify for tax-exempt status, an organization must file a list of names of people who have agreed to fulfill the legal requirements of board membership. The board members ensure that the organization operates within state and federal law, earns its money appropriately and spends it responsibly, and adopts programs most conducive to carrying out the mission of the organization.

Ask which participants are presently members of a nonprofit board or have been board members in the past. Ask them to describe the specific roles and responsibilities of board members. As they speak, write their answers on the flipchart. They should include the following:

• Setting organizational policy and reviewing and evaluating organizational plans.

• Ensuring organizational continuity. The board must develop leadership within itself and in the staff, and have a process of bringing in new leaders from outside the immediate circle of the board and staff to maintain a mix of old and new in both spheres.

- Managing personnel. The board sets and reviews personnel policies, and hires and (if necessary) fires the executive director. Generally, the board delegates the hiring and firing of other staff to the executive director. The board is also the final arbiter of staff grievances and should pay close attention to maintaining good staff-board relationships.

- Ensuring fiscal accountability. The board approves and closely monitors the organization's expenses and income. The board makes certain that all the organization's resources, including the time of volunteers and staff as well as money, are used wisely.

- Funding the organization. The board is responsible for the continued funding and financial health of the organization. From the point of view of fundraising, board members have two responsibilities: give money themselves and raise money from others.

Your group may come up with other roles and responsibilities, but it is important for you to make sure these roles are mentioned, as all other roles will be subsumed under one of these categories.

Building a Fundraising Team   (Presentation; 10 minutes)

Helping participants create a team to carry out fundraising tasks is a critical step; fundraising cannot be done effectively without a team.

> Since fundraising works best if done within a team, it's important to go about forming a team that understands its responsibilities and uses the team members so that each one is most effective. We will be reviewing a number of guidelines for forming a fundraising team. As we do, keep in mind these questions:
>
> - How can volunteers be held accountable for work they agree to do?
> - How can the guidelines balance the need for volunteers to complete tasks they have agreed to do with the fact that they have busy lives and competing priorities, which sometimes have to take precedence?

Using the flipchart, write each guideline as you present it, and then use the comments here to walk participants through the guidelines. Allow participants to spend a few moments discussing how each guideline can be applied to their specific project. Participants are creating guidelines for their fundraising efforts now; they are not filling in all the tasks, because they are not known yet. As you take participants through the next eight sessions, they will see what tasks are required for each fundraising strategy. In Session 14, they will decide on a final fundraising plan and then fill in all the tasks that the guidelines call for.

The purpose of these guidelines is to encourage the members of your organization who are participating in this class to coalesce into a team. From now on, they are not simply participants in a class but are listening for what their individual role in the group might be, and what they will recommend the group take on.

Guidelines for Forming a Fundraising Team A team is a group of people who understand the rules of the game and know which place they are playing. A fundraising team needs to establish these rules and places for everyone to work most effectively together.

> First, agree on the fundraising plan and the tasks within it. (The fundraising plan is put together in Session 14.) If people are not in agreement with the overall plan or feel that the tasks required to complete the plan are not accurate, they will not give their best effort in implementing the plan.
>
> Second, divide up the tasks such that they play to people's strengths and desires. It is less important that the work be divided up evenly than that each person feels that he can complete his assignment. Some tasks are going to be harder than others, and some are going to take longer than others, but it is important that everyone on the team feel that each person is carrying a share of the load and that no one is carrying too much or too little. Further, some people have more time to put into the project than others, and some people are more efficient in their use of time than others.
>
> Third, provide a regular way for team members to report back on their progress or problems. The simplest reporting method is through brief meetings of the whole team. Phone calls, written tracking forms, and reporting to team captains who then confer with each other can also work. The reporting method depends on the tasks, but the team must agree on a method before beginning to work.
>
> Finally, agree that people who are not completing their tasks will be confronted. Nothing demoralizes a team effort faster than one or two people who consistently don't get their work done. If someone doesn't complete a task in the time she has agreed to, ask her how she wants to proceed, and if she wishes to be relieved

of this task. Approach this problem with the Quaker attitude: "Assume good intent." If she simply took on too much or something else in her family or job has had to take priority, she needs to be able to give up her place on the team with dignity. If she needs more time or help to complete the task, that has to be negotiated.

After presenting these four guidelines, ask the group if there is anything else they would add. Point out that a congregation or ministry program is familiar with the need to have reliable volunteers. The Sunday school teachers, the ushers, the treasurer, the lay leaders who design the service while the rabbi is on leave, the carpool drivers who pick up residents from the senior center and bring them to church, and dozens of others involved in the program are already volunteers. If being on the fundraising committee is understood to be as important as carrying out any other kind of lay leadership, then forming a team that works well should not be too difficult.

Wrap-up

With this session, we finish the overview of fundraising basics that we started with Session 1. We now have the grounding we need to learn the practical details of fundraising.

With the next session, we begin to understand the details of common fundraising strategies and practical application of these strategies.

To prepare ourselves for the next session, we have some simple homework. Collect any mail appeals and special-event invitations you receive before the next session. Also, keep track of all the ways you are asked for donations between now and the next session, and note what works for you and what doesn't.

Key Learnings

What are the key learnings?

1. _____

2. _____

3. _____

Evaluation

Did this session meet its goals?

PART TWO * * * * * * * * * *

Choosing the Appropriate Strategy

YOU AND THE PARTICIPANTS are now familiar with the basic infrastructure required for effective fundraising. In the next seven sessions, you introduce participants to specific strategies. In Part One, the exercises and discussion validated their experiences and drew on knowledge they already had. Participants worked together to clarify their vision for their group and to begin to see themselves working in fundraising as a team.

The two most important elements for you to convey to participants during the next seven sessions are that (1) fundraising is a volume business and (2) the most commonly heard word in fundraising is no.

Fundraising is a volume business. It depends for success on asking many more people than the number of gifts you need. How many more people you must ask depends on what strategy you pick, as you will see in the next few chapters. The Christian testament has a story that illustrates volume in this regard: the story of the sower planting seed. Jesus tells the story in the Gospel of Matthew this way:

> A sower went out to sow. As he sowed, some seed fell along the footpath; and the birds came and ate it up. Some seed fell on rocky ground where it had little soil, and it sprouted quickly because it had no depth of earth, but when the sun rose the young corn was scorched, and as it had no root, it withered away. Some seed fell among the thistles; and the thistles shot up and choked the corn. And some of the seed fell into good soil, where it bore fruit, yielding a hundredfold or sixtyfold or thirtyfold [NEV, 13:3–9].

The lesson here is that no one can expect all the seeds she plants to bear fruit, and no one can expect all the people she asks to give money. In fundraising, it is not always clear what the rocky ground is, or where the thistles are. Like the sower, we try to aim our message to people who would be interested, but we sometimes miss.

The most important thing you as the leader can convey to the participants is this concept. Then they can ask, and let go of the need for a positive answer. If you ask enough people, you will get the money you need. Sometimes the people you most imagine giving say no, and sometimes money comes from surprising sources. This is what makes fundraising fascinating: Who will say yes? Who will say no? Who will say no and change his mind and send money? Who will say yes and change her mind and not send money? Most religious traditions teach that judgment is something best left to God, who is the only one who knows all the facts. Here is where fundraising becomes a spiritual practice; we are not to judge those who don't give. We are simply to keep asking—keep moving through our list.

The second concept—that most people say no—is obviously a corollary to the first. Since most people say no, and since we don't know ahead of time who exactly will say no, we must ask as wide a swath of people as we can. We narrow our requesting to people who we think share our values and care about our group, and to people who give away money; but even then, those who share our values may have other organizations they support and so they cannot take on our group as well. They may have other financial burdens we know nothing about, or they may have to confer with a spouse or partner. If you can find out why the person said no, you may be able to turn the no into a yes, but you need to convey to everyone you ask that he is free to turn you down and that you will not love him less for not giving.

As people working for religious organizations, we have an obligation to model behavior that is in keeping with the tenets of our tradition. In our writing and our speaking, our fundraising must support our message and not contradict it. How we ask, how we receive, how we give, how we appreciate, and how we accept rejection are all observed as part of our work. As the leader, you must model this behavior as well as convey it.

The next seven sessions continue to draw on participant experience, but there will be times when a participant's personal feelings about a strategy are not helpful in understanding it. For example, many participants say that they dislike receiving direct mail or being phoned at home. They have to see that their personal dislike of these strategies does not mean the strategies are not useful.

As you look at each strategy, you must draw people away from their personal likes and dislikes to look at the strategy in a larger way. The more familiar they become with each of the strategies listed, the more they are able to do that. You may also wish to consider bringing in to any of these sessions guest speakers who have deeper experience with the strategies. Participants use the information they learn in the seven sessions of Part Two to create a fundraising plan, so it is critical they have an accurate understanding of each strategy, and of the way the strategies work together in an overall plan.

SESSION 6 ✳ ✳ ✳ ✳ ✳ ✳ ✳ ✳ ✳ ✳

Overview of Fundraising Strategies and Their Uses

OVERVIEW OF SESSION

Goals   At the end of this session, participants will:

1. Understand the purpose and value of each fundraising strategy

2. Know how to choose fundraising strategies appropriate to the goal

3. Know what results to expect from each fundraising strategy

Methodology   Presentation and discussion, individual presentations to the group

Time   Thirty minutes to prepare, one hour to present

SESSION 6

Content

WELCOME EVERYONE to this session. Thank people who did the homework assignments. Ask if there are any questions or concerns left over from the session on volunteers. Introduce new people, and bring up to date anyone who has missed a session.

Introduction   (Presentation; 1 Minute)

We're beginning the second phase of our fundraising course. Up to now, we've reviewed facts about fundraising: how much money is given away every year, by whom, and to what; what our attitudes toward money are, and how we got those attitudes; what fundraising is really about; and what we need to know about our organization and have in place to begin an effective fundraising program.

For the next six sessions, we'll look at several fundraising strategies in depth. In this session, we are introduced to all the grassroots strategies that organizations like ours use; then we learn how to choose the appropriate strategy or combination of strategies to meet our fundraising goals and objectives.

Being Asked for Money   (Discussion; 10 minutes)

Ask participants to note in their workbooks (page 27) and then share how they were asked for money since the last session. They can show the mail appeals they brought in (which, if people agree, should be collected for use in Session 9, on direct mail). Ask them to reflect on which of the following factors is most important in making a decision for or against giving the money:

- Timing of the request
- Believing in or knowing about the cause
- Method of request (direct mail, canvass, phone, asked by a friend)
- Pending requests from other groups
- Whether or not you feel you have the money to give
- Other (participants should name additional factors)

The group is probably divided as to which factor is most important, but many of them will say "timing" or "feeling I have the money to give" (which is often a subset of timing). Point out that as the asker, there is little you can do about timing, except to be respectful.

Effectiveness of Fundraising Strategies
(Discussion and Presentation; 30 minutes)

To finish up this group sharing, ask the participants to respond to this question: "Why does an organization choose one fundraising strategy over another?"

Answers may include:

- Purpose of the strategy (raise money, bring in new people, build community)

- Availability of time and volunteers

- Appropriateness of the strategy to the amount of money to be raised

- Ability to build on what we know

> To be deliberate about choosing a strategy requires knowing something about all the strategies, and that's what we look at in this session.
>
> It's obvious that all fundraising takes time. When you put time into fundraising, one of the things you want to get back (which is sometimes the *main* thing you want to get back) is money. Using the criterion "time in for money back," let's look at a list of strategies, ranked from most effective to least effective. As we do, reflect on your own experiences with the strategies, as a fundraiser or a donor.

Use the flipchart to write the italicized short forms, as in Table 6.1, so that everyone can see them.

> We look first at the *personal strategies*:
>
> - *Face-to-face solicitation.* If you ask someone for a gift in person and she is someone who gives away money, who cares about your cause, and whom you know personally, you have about a 50 percent chance of getting it. Of all the people you know who give away money and who you are certain care about your cause, how many do you have to ask in person to get the gift you want? (The answer is called the prospect-to-donor ratio because it tells you how many prospects are

TABLE 6.1

Effectiveness of Fundraising Strategies

Strategy	Response	Prospect-to-Donor Ratio
Personal:		
Face-to-face	50% yes 50% less than amount asked for	2:1 (for gift of specific size, 4:1)
Personal phone call	15–20%	5:1
Personal letter	10–15%	10:1
Impersonal:		
Door-to-door canvass	12%	8:1
Phone-a-thon	5%	20:1
Direct mail	10%	100:1
Special event	Depends on event	Depends on event

required for each donor; accordingly it helps you greatly in planning.) The correct answer is two: on average, one agrees to give and one doesn't. You have another 50 percent chance that the person who actually agrees gives you less than what you ask for, which means that to get a gift of a specific size, you need to ask three or four people: one or two say no, one gives less, and one gives the gift that is requested.

- *Personal phone call.* If you call someone whom you know to ask for a gift, someone who you know cares about the cause and gives away money, you have a 15-20 percent chance of getting the gift.
- *Personal letter.* If you write to someone who meets these criteria but you do not follow up with a phone call, you have a 10-15 percent chance of getting the gift.

Clearly, the closer you get to the person, the greater your chances of getting the gift.

Ask the group to reflect on why this would be, and what this kind of fundraising is similar to. Often participants compare it to looking for a job, dating, or finding a house or apartment. The similarities include volume of contacts, persistence, and personal attention.

Continue with the *impersonal strategies*:

- *Canvassing.* You may be familiar with two kinds of canvassing: door-to-door in a neighborhood, and the "all-member" canvass in which each congregant is asked to make a yearly pledge. In a door-to-door canvass, volunteers (or paid canvassers) go to each house in a neighborhood and present a brief description of the work and ask for money. School children often use this method to raise money for band uniforms or to go to camp; they may canvass by selling candy bars or magazine subscriptions. No matter how it's done, a canvass generally results in a gift or purchase at one in every eight houses, or 12 percent of the time. The all-member canvass has a much higher return, depending on how it's organized, because the people being approached are already part of the organization.

- *Phone-a-thons.* In this strategy, an organization creates or acquires a list of people whom they probably don't know, but who give to a similar organization or a related cause, and they call this list to ask these people to join their group. Generally, the response to this strategy is about 5 percent; in other words, five gifts result from every one hundred calls. The prospect-to-donor ratio is 20:1.

- *Direct mail.* Here an organization takes a list similar to the one for a phone-a-thon and writes to the people on it rather than calling them. The expected response is 1 percent, or one gift for every one hundred letters. The prospect-to-donor ratio is 100:1.

- *Special events.* An organization uses a combination of these strategies to bring people together for a party, a speech, an auction, a movie, or some happening at a specific time. Events can raise—or lose—a lot of money. They are risky and time-intensive but are often fun and potentially lucrative.

Ask people to notice the volume nature of all of these strategies.

How does it feel to say, "I'm going to call one hundred people to find five gifts" instead of "I'm going to get turned down over and over and hardly anybody will give me money"? How about approaching fundraising with the attitude that you can measure your success in part by how many people say no—that some people must say no in order for you to know that you're asking enough people? Does that change your feelings about asking?

Note also how some of the strategies appeal to the donor's belief in the cause directly, and some of them appeal to the donor's desire to get something else that helps support the cause. Giving $10 to an event that costs the organization $5 per attendee to produce may allow the donor to see a movie and feel he's made a contribution to a good cause. Giving $10 to a friend who requests it on behalf of the group results in most of the $10 going to the organization (minus the cost of the thank-you note, newsletter, or other donor benefits). A request that gives the donor a tangible reward (candy bar, auction item, baked goods) appeals to donors who don't know that much about your group and should be used to attract them. Those who care about your organization do not need (and may not want) tangible rewards for supporting you.

Thinking Beyond Money   (Brainstorm; 10 Minutes)

In this exercise, you can go through as many strategies as you want and time allows, listing participants' answers on the flipchart. What participants see is that each strategy does some things well and some things badly.

> Fundraising takes time. The list we've just created reflects wanting money to come out of the time put in. Thinking beyond money now, what do you want for your time if you're doing special events?

Usual answers include:

- Fun
- Building community
- Bringing in new people
- Visibility
- Publicity
- Raising money from people who wouldn't give otherwise

> What do you want for your time if you're doing direct mail?

Usual answers include:

- Acquiring new donors
- Educating a broad community

- Giving people a message about your group that they can read at their convenience in their own home

When choosing strategies, then, we must ask these questions:

1. How much money do we want to make?

2. How much money can we spend?

3. What do we want besides money (new donors, visibility, outreach, thanking volunteers, etc.)?

Homework

Ask participants to collect samples of invitations to special events, direct mail appeals, or other related material and bring them to the next session.

Wrap-up

Fundraising is more complicated than simply raising money. It's meeting people's needs for community and for participation in an organization doing meaningful work. It involves making donors happy that they gave their money, inviting people to be a part of the organization, involving people in working in the organization—all things we should know from our other work in our religious communities.

Since starting this course, how have we shifted in our understanding of the role of fundraising in building an organization?

In the next session, we start our in-depth review of strategies with the most popular one of all time, the one most closely associated with grassroots fundraising: the special event.

Key Learnings

What are the key learnings?

1. _____

2. _____

3. _____

Evaluation

Did this session meet its goals?

SESSION 7 ✳ ✳ ✳ ✳ ✳ ✳ ✳ ✳ ✳ ✳

Special Events

OVERVIEW OF SESSION

Goals At the end of this session, participants will:

1. Recognize that they already have a lot of experience and knowledge about special events, both from planning them and attending them

2. Know the correct use of special events

3. Be able to choose the best event for their situation based on appropriate criteria

4. Have experience working in a team to plan an event

Methodology Presentation and discussion, small groups with report-back to big group

Time Twenty minutes to prepare, one hour to present

Note • This session can be done in one hour, and there is no reason to spend more time on it. However, you have to keep people on track regarding time, especially during the report-backs at the end of the last exercise. If participants give too many details, people get bored. Be very clear about what questions the participants are to answer in front of the group.

SESSION 7

Content

WELCOME EVERYONE to the session. See if there are questions or concerns left over from the previous session. Ask if participants have any comments about how they were solicited for money since the last session. Ask them to hand in their special-event or direct mail invitations.

Introduction   (Presentation; 2 Minutes)

Holding special events is the strategy that most of you are familiar with. Almost everyone has been to a special event, and most people have been to dozens—some to hundreds. Many people have planned and put on events. So you are working with the experience of being both a consumer and a provider of events. Further, religious life is built around events, from the weekly event of the religious service to the holy days of each year. In addition, other events are part of many religious traditions: church bazaars, Sukkot festivals, Buddha's birthday. Adding a fundraising component to any of these events, where appropriate, is not difficult.

Let's look through some of the events people have been invited to.

Open and pass around a few of the special-event invitations.

Review   (Discussion; 5 Minutes)

Ask participants to share experiences with planning or attending fundraising events. Brainstorm answers to these questions (this can be done quickly because it is a review of part of the previous session):

- How would you define a special event?
- What is good about events?
- What is not so good about events?

Why Hold a Special Event   (Presentation; 2 Minutes)

In listening to what is good and what is not so good about events, it's easy to see that there are two reasons to choose an event as a fundraising strategy. The first is to raise the overall visibility of the organization or project, and the second is to raise money, either from new people or from people or places that wouldn't give us money otherwise. If your event brings in the same people who come to all your other events and who would give you money anyway in response to a letter or over the phone, then you're not using the strategy effectively. In those cases, a special event is costing more to get the same money in.

An event is best used to reach out to people who haven't given before but who might give regularly if they know about your program. It's also a way to reach out to businesses, corporations, or people who want the advantage of advertising or being publicly associated with your organization, or who want to meet the people they think will be at your event. Ad books (made by creating the program book for an event and then selling ad space in it), events that honor people, receptions, and the like reach people who wouldn't give otherwise.

Sometimes an event is also used just to reach people who like the kind of event: a dance, an auction, a movie benefit. They may not even notice who the event is benefiting. Finally, some events allow people who appreciate your organization but can only give a small donation to feel good about their gift. A $1 raffle ticket or a $7 entry fee to a movie is perfect for them.

Criteria for Choosing an Event (Presentation and Discussion; 15 Minutes)

As you go through this presentation, list the key words on the flipchart that are italicized here.

Keeping in mind what an event is for, here are some suggested criteria for choosing an event:

- Does the event promote the *image* of the group? Rather than a beer bash, a campus ministry does a $7 all-you-can-eat spaghetti dinner to reach out to new students. A Zen retreat center, promoting the benefits of meditation, does a guided meditation lecture rather than a rock-and-roll concert.
- Do we have enough *volunteers* for the amount of work required?
- Do we have the *front money* required for things like the deposit for the venue, or printing the invitations?
- Do we have enough *time* to plan the event, and is the timing of the event good? Many events take two or three months or more to plan and organize. In projecting that far, you have to think

about what religious holidays, sporting events, school vacations, and so on may conflict with the event or the tasks to plan it.

- Is the event *repeatable*? Events often take two or three years to reach their stride and generate the most publicity and money they can. A one-time-only event need not be rejected, but you must think about the pros and cons of using a lot of volunteer energy and time to create something that you can't build on.

Are there any other criteria you would add?

Ask participants if there are additional criteria that religious groups in particular should consider.

Ranking   (Small Groups; 5 Minutes)

Ask participants to form groups of three or four. Instruct them to spend five minutes naming three events they could do for their project that meet the criteria just outlined and jot them in their workbooks, page 32. Have the groups report back, and note on the flipchart what each group has come up with. The whole group then chooses the top three events they would like to consider doing.

Steps in Planning a Special Event   (Presentation; 10 Minutes)

Use the flipchart to write the outline of the master task list, the budget, and the time line.

There are four steps to planning a special event.

1. Form an event committee of four or five people who coordinate the event. They plan it and then delegate most of the tasks to a much larger group of people. The event committee should be a small, tightly knit group of people who work well together, who want to be accountable to each other, and who are not afraid to hold other people accountable for what they volunteer to do.

    The committee carries out the next three steps:

2. Create the master task list.
3. Create a budget.
4. Create a time line.

The master task list has four columns. (See the sample in Table 7.1, at the end of this session, page 76.) Participants have this task list on page 33.

The task list details what has to be done, by when, and who is going to do it; the list offers a space to record when it actually gets done. The master task list is a living document; if used properly it yields easy-to-see information on what remains to be done, who is reliable and who isn't, and areas in which the committee is behind or ahead in its planning.

The budget (see the example in Table 7.2 page 77; page 34 in participant's workbook) has column headings in two sets that allow you to easily compare income and expenses (costs), both estimated and actual.

To create a budget, go through the master task list and write down everything that's going to cost money. Those are your expenses. Now, carefully detail everything that raises money. That's your income. See if the relationship between projected expenses and projected income meets your goals for the event.

Remind participants at this point that sometimes an event loses money but is considered successful anyway because of visibility or publicity, or the new people it attracts.

After the event is over, the committee goes through and adds up all the actual expenses and income. This gives accurate figures for this event, but more important, the budget and the task list provide valuable and time-saving information for next year's planners.

Last is putting the task list on a time line. See the sample time line on page 78 (in the participant's workbook on page 35).

Take each task and note how many hours or days it will take to complete, and when it can start. If you don't have any idea how long something takes, you should add another task to your task list: finding out how long the task took someone who knows. Be sure to factor in that some tasks cannot be started until others are completed, and add one extra day for every five days of estimates to allow for mistakes and people being late.

By carefully adding up the number of hours and days required to get everything done, you have a clear sense of whether you can produce the event in the time you have allowed. In this process, you may think of things that should be on the task list that you have forgotten. Groups often forget this third step—to their later regret. It's a check-and-balance process to ensure that you're being realistic about your ability to do this event.

Exercise   **(Small Groups, Discussion; 35 Minutes)**

Ask participants to form groups of five people so that there are no more than four or five groups total. Ask them to choose one person (the reporter) to report back to the group after the exercise. Instruct them to take ten minutes to prepare a task list and time line for a special event. Ideally, some groups work with the events you chose earlier, but it is possible that in the discussion people have thought of other events they would rather try out.

Give each group several pieces of flipchart paper and marking pens to write their plans. Tell the group to note the process they go through, including:

- How they discuss things
- Where tensions arise and how they deal with them
- Any obstacles they run into in planning this event

At the end of the ten minutes, ask each group to hang its papers on a wall for everyone to see, and then ask the reporter to take three minutes to summarize briefly what they have planned. The reporter should tell the whole group what event her small group picked and then reflect on the process the committee engaged in, rather than the actual details of the plan. Ask them to focus on these questions:

- Was it fun?
- Did your group get a lot accomplished?
- Were you tempted to cut corners or make things up (such as, "I know we could get that donated" or "Let's pretend we know someone who owns a restaurant")?

The whole group briefly asks questions or comments on the plans of each presenting group.

After all the report-backs are done, ask people to reflect on the whole exercise and to consider, based on their experience, whether anything has been left out that someone feels needs to be mentioned.

Wrap-up

Think ahead to any special events you'll be attending before the next session. When you go, note in what ways they're well planned and how they can be improved. In the next session, we begin exploring raising money by mail.

Key Learnings

1. _____

2. _____

3. _____

Evaluation

Since you're now halfway through this course, take a few more minutes than usual for evaluation. How is the course working for everyone? Does anything need to be changed? What's working best?

SAMPLES OF STEPS IN EVENT PLANNING

Tables 7.1 and 7.2 also appear in the participant's workbook.

Master Task List

This is the beginning list. The master task list refers to other lists that spell out the details of a specific type of task, such as publicity or the ad book. Coordinators of pieces of work have their own lists, which need to be integrated into the master list so that everyone involved is confident that everything has been thought of and that work is not being duplicated.

TABLE 7.1

Sample Master Task List for Special Event: Dinner and Auction 9/25. Today's date: 3/1.

What	When (Deadline)	Who	Date Done
Secure church hall	3/15	Marcie	
Draft budget	3/20	Marcie and Ellen	
Get bids from three caterers	3/20	Ellen	
Choose caterer	3/30	Committee	
Create auction committee to solicit auction items	4/1	Marianne	
Committee creates time lines and list of desirable items	4/25	Marianne and Tom	
Create publicity committee	4/1	Arturo and Randy	
Committee creates time line and budget; present to master committee	4/25		
Budget finalized	4/25	Marcie and committee	
Ask Harley to be auctioneer	4/1	Tim	
Ask Gary and Jan to emcee	4/1	Tim	
(Make list of other options if they can't)	4/10	Tim and Randy	
Begin securing lists for invitation; goal is 1,000 names	4/10–6/15	Marianne and Randy	
Decide whether to serve liquor	5/1	Tim, with church board	
If yes, create budget for cash bar			

TABLE 7.2

Sample Budget for Special Event: Dinner and Auction. Date:

EXPENSES

Item	Estimated	Actual	Notes
Rental of facility			
Child care workers			
Security and janitorial			
Food and beverage			
Caterer			
Equipment rental			
Bartenders (no. of people ___ @ $___ per hr.)			
Paper products for serving			
Printing and graphics			
Invitations			
Tickets			
Posters and signage			
Programs			
Copying			
Publicity			
Photographer			
Paid ads			
Complimentary tickets			
Mailing house			
Postage			
Donor solicitation			
Thank-you notes			
Invitations			
Miscellaneous correspondence			
Decorations			
Insurance			
Other			
Totals			

INCOME

Item	Estimated	Actual	Notes
Tickets (no. of tickets ___ @ $___ each)			
Cash donations			
Cash bar			
Auction income			
Product sales			
Other (specify)			
Totals			

GRAND TOTALS

Total net profit or loss

In-kind donations (value)

Time Line

Here is an example of three sets of tasks for the dinner-and-auction event that need to be related using a time line:

1. Invitation

2. Solicitation of auction items

3. Volunteer training

The invitation tasks, and estimates of the time required, are:

Design and approval of design	1 week
Proofreading of final copy	1 day
Printing of invitation	2 weeks
Organizing mailing party (while invitation is being printed)	3 hours
Mailing party, to mail to 1,000 names	2 evenings
Total time for invitation	Almost 4 weeks

The tasks and time estimates for soliciting auction items are:

Compile list of desirable items	1 day
Prepare materials for merchants	1 week

- Copy letter of tax exemption

- Create brochure

- Create sample of program book where merchants' names (ads) will appear

- Contract for getting auction item

- Folder

Training volunteers to be auction item solicitors involves these tasks and times:

Prepare materials for solicitors	1 week

- Question-and-answer sheet

- Sample script

- List of places to solicit items)

Schedule training	3 days
Conduct training	1 evening
Total time for getting solicitors ready	10 days

SESSION 8 ✳ ✳ ✳ ✳ ✳ ✳ ✳ ✳ ✳ ✳

The Wide World of Mail

OVERVIEW OF SESSION

Goals

At the end of this session, participants will:

1. Understand the purpose of direct mail and the meaning of donor acquisition

2. Understand how to use mail to keep donors interested in giving

3. Have the tools to evaluate making a decision to spend money to make money

4. Know how to obtain effective mailing lists

Methodology

Lecture and discussion, group work, individual work with report-back to the group

Time

Thirty minutes to prepare; one hour to present

Note

- You may find participants becoming more confused in this session than in any previous one. Move slowly through the material, stopping frequently to make sure everyone is following.

SESSION 8

Content

WELCOME EVERYONE to this session. Ask if there are questions or concerns about the last session on special events. If anyone missed that session, ask participants to share the most important learnings. Once people are settled, begin with the opening discussion.

Introduction   (Discussion; 5 Minutes)

Hold up a sampling of direct mail appeals. Ask people to imagine they are at home, not in an analytical mode as they are here. Ask:

- Is any of these one that you would open?

- How do you choose which appeals you open and which you throw away?

Help the group notice that people have differing reactions to types of mail. Some common reactions:

- I only open mail from groups I'm familiar with.

- Sometimes I open a piece of mail because I'm in a good mood, or I'm delaying doing something like fixing dinner.

- I never open junk mail.

- I open mail if it says I get a free gift, like mailing labels or a bumper sticker.

- I open a letter if I can't tell who it's from, because I'm curious.

- Direct mail offends me because it wastes trees and causes pollution.

Close this discussion with the following comment:

> People have a lot of reactions to direct mail, but everyone is familiar with it. Apart from special events, it's the most common form of fundraising, generating more than $60 billion a year in donations. So it is effective.

What's Good About Direct Mail?   (Brainstorm; 10 Minutes)

Have the group brainstorm the answers to these questions while you jot their comments on the flipchart:

- Why is direct mail so successful?

- What is good about direct mail?

Answers usually include:

- Cheap to send

- Easy to respond to

- Gives a person something to look over in her own home

- Can be educational

- A way to keep in touch with donors

  Some optional questions:

- Can you give examples of organizations you have worked with that had good experiences with direct mail?

- How about bad experiences?

Direct Mail for Donor Acquisition (Presentation; 15 minutes)

Drawing upon our reactions as consumers of direct mail, and as people who've used it, we can see there is a wide range of opinions about direct mail. Let's start our lesson with looking at the purposes of direct mail.

Organizations use direct mail to accomplish two things. they want to bring in new donors, or they want to communicate with donors they already have and ask them to give again. Direct mail is generally not used for soliciting large gifts and cannot be used where a personal touch is needed.

Donor acquisition—getting someone to give for the first time—is the primary purpose of direct mail, and it's the most efficient way to reach large numbers of people with one message. Here's how it works.

Write the statistics that occur in the next narrative on the flipchart or blackboard as you speak.

Let's take a group as an illustration. The Peace and Justice Center is a joint project of five churches and two synagogues; the center has decided to experiment with direct mail to raise some money. They contact the Disarmament Project, a secular group opposed to maintaining nuclear arsenals and military spending. The Peace and Justice Center has collaborated with this group in the past and thinks that their members would agree with the programs of the center.

The groups propose to trade mailing lists. Each group has one thousand donors. After purging the duplicates (people who already belong to both groups) they have about nine hundred names each. The Peace and Justice Center sends out nine hundred letters asking people to join at $35 (or more) and gets a 1 percent response—the standard for direct mail.

One percent of nine hundred requests equals nine donations. The total income is one gift at $100, one at $75, two at $50, and five at $35, or $450 from nine people.

It costs the Peace and Justice Center 60 cents each to send out these letters. This includes printing costs, the postage, and the $30 they paid two teenagers to put the appeal together and get it ready for bulk mail. Thus 900 pieces at 60 cents each means the cost of the mailing is $540.

Although it looks as if this mailing lost $90 ($450 minus $540), what's actually true is that the Peace and Justice Center spent $90 to acquire nine donors, or $10 per donor. If they write to these people again in six months or so, and just three of the recipients give again at, say, only $30 or $35, the group more than makes back its money on the original mailing. The $90 is an investment in beginning a relationship with these nine people.

Of course, on occasion a targeted mailing does better than a 1 percent response, or more people send in $50 or more. But for planning and projecting purposes, it's always better to follow the wisdom that the happiest fundraisers project costs high and income low.

Generally, about 66-75 percent of people renew their gifts every year, so the Peace and Justice Center can expect six of these nine people to give over and over again. Perhaps one of them will become a major donor, giving $250, $500, or more. It's obvious that this only happens if the Peace and Justice Center is willing to write to these donors several times and become personally acquainted with at least some of them.

More than any other strategy, direct mail illustrates the grassroots fundraising principle that if you aren't willing or able to follow through on your fundraising, you might as well not start it in the first place. It's like making a cake: you can mix up the ingredients, but if you don't bake it, you won't have the final product you set out to produce.

Groups should add to their annual budgets a line item for "acquisition" and plan to spend some amount of money each year acquiring donors.

Make sure everyone understands the principle of *acquisition*. Use this optional exercise, or ask a suitable participant to teach the class the principle of acquisition in her own words.

Investing (Optional Brainstorm; 5 Minutes)

What examples from our lives can we come up with that require investing in something and waiting on the return? What are the considerations that go into such a decision? How do we evaluate how much to risk?

Answers to the first question—examples of investing and waiting for return—might include:

- Investing in stocks
- Buying a house
- Obtaining an advanced education
- Starting a small business
- Moving to a new location

Mailing Lists Are Key (Presentation, Brainstorm; 5 minutes)

A 1 percent return is not guaranteed on direct mail programs. Organizations sometimes send out direct mail and get a 0 percent response and so lose all their investment. Organizations have also sent out direct mail and gotten a 2 percent, 3 percent, or even 5 percent response. The main variable in whether we get zero response or something much higher is the quality of the lists we use.

Think of a time when you responded to a direct mail appeal from a group you had not given to before. In other words, you were among the 1 percent return. What made you a good candidate for them?

Common answers:

- Believed in a similar cause
- Wanted to do something about issue for some time

- Knew and respected someone who was involved
- Have a hard time resisting pictures of animals, children, etc.

From these answers, what can we learn about what makes a list good to use?

Emphasize that belief in a similar cause, or belief or admiration for a particular person or celebrity, are big factors—as is emotion—in deciding to respond to a mail appeal.

Types of Mailing Lists   (Presentation; 10 Minutes)

There are three kinds of list for direct mail:

Hot. People on a hot list are characterized by two things: they know about your group, and they care about your cause. The most sizzling hot list, of course, is people who are already donors. The second-hottest list is people who are friends of donors. Writing to current donors once a year asking for names of people who might be interested generally yields a very good list.

Warm. People on a warm list are characterized by one of the same two things: they either know about your group or care about the cause, but we can't say for sure they do both. Warm-list prospects might include the following groups:

- People who may have had a good experience with your group (or maybe not)
- People who give to similar groups: they care about the cause but perhaps don't know about your group
- People who attend your special events: maybe they love the event but don't care about your group; maybe they love your group and think the event is a way to get on your mailing list or support you in a small way
- People who call for more information
- People who used to give but no longer do

Any others?

Cold. People on a cold list are those we know nothing about. Mail sent to "current resident" is cold mail.

Where to Get Lists   (Brainstorm; 5 Minutes)

Ask the group to brainstorm the answers to the question, "Where can we get warm or hot lists for our project?"

Remind them that they need two hundred names to qualify for the discount allowed for bulk mail; however, for a list that is hot enough they might want to consider sending the mailing first class.

Among the ideas that usually emerge:

- Approach friends of all the people in this group.
- Write to our current donors.
- Ask others in our congregation for names.
- Ask friends who are active in similar organizations for names.
- Ask all the people who come to our events.
- Go to people in the neighborhood.

Add this note about using other organizations' mailing lists:

> Sometimes people are hesitant about giving out names of their donors. If you're concerned that your donors may not wish their names to be shared with other groups, you can include a checkbox in all your return correspondence and the comment, "From time to time we trade mailing lists with other organizations that we think our donors would be interested in. If you would rather we did not trade your name, please check here."
>
> Very few donors check this box, but those who do are pulled from any list that's traded. Even though people complain about the volume of direct mail they receive, many people also learn a lot from the appeals they get; experienced fundraisers have discovered that, if given the choice to receive them or not, most people choose to receive them.

Wrap-up

Review the lessons learned from this session, and tell participants that the next session continues with the details of creating a direct mail appeal.

Key Learnings

1. _____
2. _____
3. _____

Evaluation

Did this session meet its goals?

SESSION 9 ✳ ✳ ✳ ✳ ✳ ✳ ✳ ✳ ✳ ✳

The Direct Mail Package

OVERVIEW OF SESSION

Goals At the end of this session, participants will:

1. Understand the parts of a direct mail appeal

2. Know how to craft a direct mail appeal

3. Have practice writing a direct mail letter

Methodology Lecture and discussion, group work, individual work with report-back to the group

Time Thirty minutes to prepare; 60–90 minutes to present

Note • Bring the mail appeals from Session 8 and any others you have collected.

SESSION 9

Content

WELCOME EVERYONE to this session. Ask if there are questions about the last session on direct mail.

Ask a participant to explain again the concept of acquisition.

After people are settled, remind them that in the last session they learned how to create or acquire effective mailing lists to which to send their mail appeals. Explain that this session dissects the elements of a successful mail appeal.

Four Key Components   (Discussion; 15 Minutes)

Pass around the appeals for people to open. Ask them to name the four components that all the appeals have:

1. The outside envelope

2. The letter itself

3. A reply device (sometimes the return envelope has a large back flap and the reply device is printed there; these church-style envelopes are called "wallet envelopes")

4. A return envelope

   Ask if any of the letters have other components. Possibilities include:

- Newspaper clippings

- Address labels

- Testimonial notes

- Bookmarks

- Bumper stickers

   Ask the group to reflect on the function of each of the four main components and jot their responses on the flipchart. You can draw the conclusions discussed next from what people say (or guide them to these conclusions in the rare instance that they get off track).

Outside Envelope The outside envelope says "Open me." Maybe it says "This letter is interesting (or is useful, or has free stuff, or is funny, or is important)."

The Letter The main purpose of the letter is to arouse an emotion and to suggest that the appropriate expression of that emotion is to make a donation.

Fundraisers often observe that people buy with their hearts first and then their heads. The emotion is created by stories, pictures, or declamatory sentences, and by involving the reader through repeating the word *you.*

Reply Device   The reply device allows the reader to respond easily. Notice that all reply devices switch voice to the first person. Whereas the letter talks to "you," the reply device says, "I'll help," "Count me in," or "I want to make a difference."

Return Envelope   The return envelope is a convenience for the donor: self-addressed, the right size for a check, requiring only a stamp, and sometimes not even that.

Analysis of an Appeal   (Pairs; 10 Minutes)

Divide the group into pairs and have each pair consider one direct mail letter from the packages they have opened. Ask the pairs to spend two minutes with the letter, noting how it is structured. Each pair then shares observations with the whole group.

Note people's observations on the flipchart. They often include:

- Opening sentence or paragraph is a story that grabs your interest.
- The middle has more stories, facts, and details about the issue and what the group is doing about the issue.
- Possibly in the beginning, but definitely at the end, the letter asks for money—usually specific amounts for specific things.
- The letter is signed by one person, possibly someone famous or having credentials to make him or her more believable.
- The letter almost always has a P.S., and possibly more than one.
- The letter may make use of bullets, stars, underlining, boldface, and other formatting devices to draw the eye to a particular point.
- Paragraphs are short.
- The letter is two, three, or four pages.
- It's easy to read, although not well written in a literary sense.

Ask which, among the things they have noticed, they can use in their letters. Answers might include:

- Stories
- Letter signed by one person

- Postscript
- Asking for specific amounts
- Telling about our group and what we have done
- Short paragraphs
- Two pages

Anatomy of a Direct Mail Letter   (Presentation; 10 Minutes)

The majority of people read three parts of a direct mail letter: the opening paragraph, the closing paragraph, and the postscript. Up to 60 percent of them decide whether to give based on those three parts and don't read the rest of the letter.

You're probably wondering, then, why most direct mail appeals are two, three, or four pages. Research has shown over and over that longer letters tend to do better than shorter ones. This is because the letter has to convey a sense of being important, and we tend to think of longer letters as more important and thoughtful. The letter has to convey respect for the reader, which many think a short letter does not do. Plus, there are some readers who read more of the letter, and some who read the whole thing, so there must be enough information to satisfy that group as well.

Grassroots organizations have generally found that a two-page letter works well, using the front and back of one sheet of paper, and they don't need to go to a longer one. Although some groups have succeeded with just one page, two pages give you room to tell more about your group or project and to make the letter readable and attractive, with space between lines and wide margins. Keep in mind that many people wear glasses and they will not make the effort to read small type squashed onto a page.

Your sentences should be short and interesting. People read these letters voluntarily, taking time out of their busy days. They demand to know quickly what you want and why they should be interested. If you think about how quickly people make decisions about how to use time, you get a sense of how much time you have in your appeal to hold attention. Think of channel surfing with your remote control, deleting words and sentences on your computer, deciding to pick up the phone or let a machine answer, when to pull out into traffic, or even whether to greet a stranger on the street or pass the person quickly. Our days are filled with decisions that are made very quickly, almost unconsciously. Direct mail is going to be reviewed at that speed.

Let's look at the anatomy of a direct mail letter.

Opening Paragraph

The opening paragraph is used to tell a story. The story can be about someone you have helped, or it can be about the person reading the letter. It needs to end positively. Take a minute to read the sample openings in your workbook on page 42.

From a campus minister:

> Dear Friend,
>
> Mary came to Westminster House a few weeks ago. She sobbed out a story of rejection: since she came out as a lesbian, her parents have disowned her and her sorority sisters have asked her to move out. I reassured her that God loves her, and that the people rejecting her are simply frightened. In a group session with the members of her sorority and in family sessions with her parents, Mary has been able to express her pain at their rejection, and both her parents and her friends are realizing that there is nothing wrong with her.

From an Israeli and Palestinian day camp:

> *You are not required to do everything, nor can you shrink from doing your part.*
> *The Talmud*
>
> Dear Friend,
>
> Do you, like me, wonder what part you play in making peace in the Middle East? I believe there are many answers. At our camp, we have one of them: bring young people together and let them talk to each other. Here's what two campers had to say:
>
>> I'd never talked to a Palestinian before. I discovered that we want many of the same things, and that our differences can make us interesting to each other, not enemies of each other. (Rahel, age 14)
>>
>> My father is a Palestinian and my mother is an Israeli. I've always been embarrassed by this, but after being at this camp, I'm proud to be both of these things. (Samir, age 16)

From a food bank:

> Dear Friend:
>   A woman asked me recently, "What do you do at the Food Bank?"
>   "We feed people," I said.
>   "Is that all?" she asked, but after a few seconds of silence she added, "That's a lot, isn't it?"

All of these opening words are designed to intrigue, provoke feelings, and catch attention. They don't tell you much about the group, or provide much rationale for the work the group has chosen to do. That comes later in the letter.

Closing Paragraph

The closing paragraph tells people what you would like them to do. It's straightforward and clear. Again, look at the examples of closing paragraphs in your workbook.

> Please take a moment now to make a gift of $35, $50, $100, or whatever you can afford. Send it in the enclosed envelope.

> We can provide a year's worth of school supplies to a child at our mission school for only $2.40. Will you consider buying the supplies for a classroom of fifteen children for $36? A card and envelope are enclosed for your convenience.

Some religious traditions are opposed to suggesting specific amounts of money. Those groups can use phrases such as these:

> Please consider prayerfully what you can give.

> I hope you will join me in making a gift to this important ministry. Whatever you can give will be put right to work.

The Postscript

The P.S. part of the letter can be used in many ways, but it's usually to encourage immediate action. Promising a reward for acting quickly is very effective:

> If we receive your donation by December 1, we will send you a free booklet, titled "Feminist Prayers for Every Occasion," compiled by the Women's Circle of our church.

> A generous donor has given us $5,000, which we must match by Rosh Hashanah. Please send your donation now to ensure that we meet this match.

If we can raise $30,000 by April 30, our congregation can promise a family in substandard housing a new house by the end of the summer.

Body of the Letter

People often wonder what goes into the rest of the letter. (Do they wonder this because they don't read them?) The answer is as varied as direct mail itself: more stories, plans for the future, statements of philosophy—whatever you feel best promotes your group. Most organizations use the bulk of the space available to show readers that their group is capable of accomplishing what they propose by telling readers what's already been accomplished. Remember what we learned in the first sessions: people buy with their heart first, then their head.

A story that touches the heart makes the reader want to know more. It inspires questions: "Who is this group? Can I trust it?" If the letter answers those questions affirmatively so that the reader says, "This is a good group. They have a solid track record," then the "head" buys. Then the reader will wonder, "What can I do to help?" So the letter starts with an appeal to the heart, continues with appeals to both head and heart, and ends by telling the reader how he or she can be part of this important work. Use the opening, closing, and postscript as the structure around which the rest of the letter is built.

Practice   (Work Alone, Pairs, Group Discussion; 15 Minutes)

Instruct the participants to spend five minutes by themselves writing an opening paragraph, a closing paragraph, and a postscript for their project on page 44 of their workbooks.

After five minutes, tell them to form pairs to share what they have written with each other and give each other feedback. After three minutes, ask two or three people to volunteer to read their opening paragraphs aloud.

Do the same with the closing paragraph and postscript.

What have you learned by writing these parts of your own appeal letter? How is an appeal letter like a sermon or a speech? Is an appeal letter like anything else that you may be familiar with?

Answers may include:

- News articles
- Press releases
- Public service announcements
- Certain kinds of reports

What Goes with the Letter?

Pull out reply devices from the direct mail appeals you have brought to class and show them to participants as you go through this section.

The final piece that we explore is the reply device. This is the card that goes in the return envelope. Since people are busier and busier, the reply device is often the part of the direct mail package they look at in any detail. The reply device is much smaller than the letter, usually not more than 3 by 7 inches. You can print on both sides of it if you want. The reply device should summarize how the reader can help. The structure is straightforward:

- YES, I want to help (or) YES, count me in.

The reply device is always written in the first person, so essentially the reader reads about his or her own behavior.

Four or five boxes suggest varying amounts. The first two boxes should name amounts most people could really give, such as $35 or $50. A third box can ask for $100 or more, and a fourth box can suggest "Other." Don't name amounts that are very low, such as $10 or $15, unless you think this is all your audience can afford; people who want to give that much will check "Other" and do so. Similarly, naming very large amounts such as $1,000 or $5,000 may put off some people, who feel that their gift is too small to make any difference. Very few people give $1,000 to a direct mail appeal, particularly if it's the first time they've ever heard about your group.

Give space for the reader to write his name and address, or to correct a label you may have put on the card. If you want, you can include two other lines:

From time to time, we share mailing lists with organizations we think our donors would be interested in. Please check here if you'd rather we did *not* share your name: ☐

We would like to thank you by listing your name in our annual report. If you'd rather remain anonymous, please check here: ☐

The Whole Package

There's no need to put anything inside an appeal letter besides the letter, the reply device, and the return envelope. Research shows that brochures tend to decrease response—and they're expensive. Newspaper articles or giveaways such as labels or bumper stickers may attract attention, but they're an unnecessary expense for grassroots organizations. Further, many religious and environmental groups point out that this is a waste of resources that we are supposed to be stewarding, and it promotes a culture of materialism that we oppose.

Ask participants if there are any final questions or concerns.

We've now examined two strategies in depth: special events and direct mail. We can see that we know more about these strategies than we may have thought, and at the same time we've had to correct some misinformation. In our next session, we look at the strategy people just love to hate: raising money by telephone.

Wrap-up

Key Learnings

1. _____

2. _____

3. _____

Evaluation

Did the session meet its goals?

Judicious Use of the Telephone

OVERVIEW OF SESSION

Goals At the end of this session, participants will:

1. Understand how the telephone fits into fundraising
2. Know how to create a script to use for fundraising on the telephone
3. Simulate asking for money over the phone

Methodology Presentation, individual work, role play

Time Thirty minutes to prepare; 60–90 minutes to present, depending on discussion

Notes • The most important element of this section is getting people to practice with each other. Allow at least twenty minutes for the practice exercise.

• Participants may be inclined to complain about telemarketers and phone scams. Move them away from this topic by having them focus on their group. Since the participants are not dishonest and are not trying to rip off vulnerable people, they don't need to worry about that. Help participants focus on how their group uses the phone, what their group says, and how their group is not like impersonal or pushy telemarketers. The more they practice here, the more they focus on the issues that help them use the phone more effectively.

- Write up the activity "Figuring the Cost Effectiveness of a Phone Campaign" (page 47 in the participant's workbook) on the flipchart or blackboard ahead of the session.

SESSION 10

Content

WELCOME EVERYONE to this session. Ask if there are questions or concerns from any of the previous sessions.

Ask if people are relating to their direct mail any differently now that they understand the psychology of it. If anyone missed the previous session, ask the group to provide highlights of it.

Introduction   (Small Groups; 2 Minutes)

Ask participants to form groups of three, then introduce the exercise:

> To learn how to use the telephone for fundraising, we have to be conscious of our attitude toward it. People who use the phone to make social plans, who converse with friends and family, and who enjoy being called by friends have a different reaction to using the telephone to raise money than those who dislike being on the phone and use it primarily as a way to learn or convey important information. Take five minutes to tell each other how you feel about the telephone?

Refer participants to the following questions you have written on the flipchart:

- How many phone lines do you have at home?
- Did you always have a phone when you were growing up?
- Do you have an answering machine? Do you remember when you got your first answering machine?
- Do you enjoy being on the telephone?

Bring participants back together. If participants' ages vary widely, point out any differences in attitude toward the telephone between seniors and younger people who have grown up with both telephones and answering machines. Explore whether there is a difference in how people feel about raising money by phone if they have call waiting, cell phones, and beepers, or if they just have one line at home. Ask if anyone in the group uses or has used the telephone as a sales or fundraising tool.

If anyone uses or has used the phone to raise money or sell something, he or she can help you help the rest of the participants understand why phoning works, even though many people dislike it.

Figuring Cost Effectiveness of a Phone Campaign   (Presentation; 30 Minutes)

Using the flipchart, take participants through the following numbers; have them refer to the corresponding page in their workbook (page 47).

> Phone campaigns work on the same principle of volume as direct mail or any other fundraising strategy. Phone campaigns work better than direct mail because of the human interaction that phoning allows.
>
> Before we learn more about how to conduct a phone-a-thon, we need to remind ourselves of the kind of response we are looking for. Look at the information in your workbook under the heading "Figuring Cost Effectiveness of a Phone Campaign."
>
> Let's say we make one hundred calls. Of these, sixty result in no answer, busy, disconnected, and so on. So forty potential prospects are reached.
>
> Of the forty, thirty refuse to hear the whole presentation. That leaves us with ten actual full contacts.
>
> Of those ten, four say no. Six say yes. Of the six who say yes, one ends up not paying.
>
> So, of one hundred calls, we have five new donors (a 5 percent response). If these five all give the requested gift of $35, we gross $175 (five times $35). Therefore, we're making $175 for every hundred attempted calls, or $1.75 per call. Since a volunteer or paid solicitor ought to be able to reach fifteen potential prospects per hour (not including answering machines, disconnects, etc.), the solicitor is bringing in $26.25 for the organization per hour of calling. With some luck, a few prospects may give $50 or $100, increasing the amount made per hour.

Remind participants of their own experience in being called. Even though they personally might be in the group of sixty who don't answer or the thirty who refuse to hear the whole pitch, five other people do not act like them.

Now, present the advantages and disadvantages of fundraising by phone, listing key ideas on the flipchart.

Advantages

1. *Most people have phones.* People are familiar with them, and with being asked for money over the phone. Phoning is safe for both the caller and the person being called. In contrast, door-to-door canvassing can be scary for the person being approached and dangerous for the person doing the canvassing.

2. *Phoning is as personal as you can get* without visiting a prospect face-to-face. We know that the main reason people give is because they're asked, and they're more likely to give if asked personally than if asked by a letter. The telephone allows us that personal touch.

3. *You can easily phone someone you don't know,* whereas it's harder to visit such a person successfully.

4. *You can make hundreds of calls in an evening,* which makes phoning a high-volume strategy second only to direct mail.

5. *You can answer questions* that a prospect has on the spot. A direct mail appeal or a TV ad may raise questions in the prospects' minds, but they have little or no way to have their questions answered. Even a simple question or a small doubt can keep a prospect from giving.

6. *Phone solicitation is increasingly regulated.* This is both an advantage and a disadvantage. The advantage is that fewer organizations are calling, so donors are more assured that those organizations that are calling are legitimate.

Disadvantages

1. Because most people have phones and it's easy to get phone numbers, *the phone has become overused for fundraising.* Some donors resent being phoned, and few people would say they like being solicited over the phone. Some telemarketers have employed unethical, or at times even illegal, methods for raising money or selling products. Guilt-inducing messages, subtle threats ("Ms. Johnson chose to give and she got a raise the next day; Mr. Murphy chose not to and his house burned down"), and strong-arm tactics have alienated even people who were previously sympathetic to this strategy.

2. The majority of people who have phones also *have phone answering machines and use them to screen for calls* they don't want to answer, including fundraising calls. You have to call a large number of people to raise a significant amount of money. Most volunteers find it discouraging to call one hundred people and have only four or five of them make a gift.

3. *Phone solicitation is increasingly regulated,* the disadvantage of which is that it requires more work to get permission to make calls, and groups have to be prepared to handle complaints about their calls.

As we can see, phoning isn't a perfect strategy, but it's very useful if used thoughtfully. There are three types of people you can use the telephone to solicit:

1. People who've never given to your group but have given to groups similar to yours. These people are asked to join for the first time.
2. People who are currently givers to your group. These people are asked for an extra gift for a special project.
3. People who used to give to your group but haven't done so in the last twelve to eighteen months. These people are called lapsed donors. They're asked to rejoin.

In other words, phoning is best used with warm or hot lists, as defined in Session 9 on direct mail. When used with these people, here's what you can expect in results:

- About 5 percent of the people being asked for the first time give by phone.
- About 15 percent of people being asked for an extra gift give by phone.
- Ten to 30 percent of people being asked to rejoin after having not given for over a year do so.

The most efficient way to use the telephone for fundraising is a phone-a-thon. It's easy to organize. Bringing everyone together in one room decreases anxiety and raises excitement. The phone-a-thon allows instant gratification when a gift is pledged, and a real sense of satisfaction when it's over. It's a good way to kick off a fund drive—the annual all-member canvass, a special effort to raise money quickly, an effort to reenroll people who may have dropped out of the group as donors, and so on. It requires several elements of preparation.

Go over the following steps of preparation, referring participants to the appropriate pages in their workbooks.

Preparing for a Phone-a-Thon   (Presentation; 5 Minutes)

1. Set a date. Pay attention to other events in your community; don't call during the last episode of a popular TV show or when people might be attending a benefit auction for another group. It seems to work best to call on a Tuesday, Wednesday, or Thursday after 6:00 P.M. and no later than 9:00 P.M., at the beginning of the month, near payday. You may want to conduct your phone-a-thon over two nights, which allows you to try on the second night to reach those people you missed on the first.

2. Find a room or rooms with several phones. Real estate or law offices, mail-order companies, and any organization that does a lot of business on the phone may be willing to let you use their phone system in the evening. You pay for toll calls and be responsible in keeping facilities neat and clean.

3. Prepare a list of people to be called. These are people in one of the categories already described. For people who've never done a phone-a-thon before, the easiest list to prepare and to use in asking is probably your current donors. Lapsed donors are also often friendly. Many let their contributions lapse by accident, or they might think they've paid already. It's rare that they stop giving because they dislike your group.

4. Once your list is complete, you can determine how many phones and how many callers you need. Estimate that one person can make thirty to thirty-five calls an hour (overall average, including no answer, answering machine, etc.) and talk to fifteen prospects. The phoning session lasts about four hours, with three hours of calling, thirty minutes of warm-up, and thirty minutes of debriefing and wrap-up, so each volunteer should be given about one hundred names to call.

Explain that you will return to this list of steps in preparing for the phone-a-thon and add to it, but first you want to look at how to keep track of information and what a script looks like.

Keeping Track of Information   (Presentation; 2 Minutes)

Your list should be set up in columns with headings across the top to include the person's name, address, phone number, and a place to write what happened on the call. Include columns to show that the caller verified the current address, sent more information if requested, and sent a thank-you for pledges received. Your list might look like this:

- Name
- Address
- Phone number
- Response
- Address verified?
- More information sent?
- Thank-you sent?
- Other

If you're using names of previous or current donors, also include a column with information on the date and size of the person's last gift. If nothing else, the volunteer caller can thank the donor for what she's already done.

The Script   (Presentation and Discussion; 20 Minutes)

The next step in preparing for a phone-a-thon is to write a script for volunteers to use in the calls.

In general, volunteers can ad lib after the second or third call, but initially a script gives them a feeling of security. Some volunteers never deviate from the script, while others only use it once. It's important that volunteers be given some flexibility in using the script, but they have to use the main components of the intended message:

- Give your name and the name of the organization.
- Ask if the prospect has a minute to talk.
- Tell the prospect *briefly* why you are calling.
- Ask for money.
- Thank the prospect for his or her response.

If the response is positive, be sure to collect the money according to your instructions (which vary depending on the group).

The script should be brief and to the point. It should discuss what to do in the most common situations but not try to address every possible scenario.

Give participants a few minutes to review the sample script on page 49 in their workbook. Discuss any questions that arise.

Sample Script

"Hello, is John Smith available?" (If John is speaking, continue.)

"My name is Vivian Volunteer, and I'm on the board of the Religious Coalition for Environmental Protection. May I speak with you for a minute?"

(*Pause.* Be respectful of the answer. If John says he can't talk now, ask if you can call back later. If he says he's not interested, say thank you nicely and hang up. If he says "I never make contributions over the phone," ask if you can send some information in the mail that he can read over to decide whether to give.)

(If he says he can talk now, continue.)

"Have you heard of the Religious Coalition for Environmental Protection?"

(If yes, the prospect will probably volunteer what he knows about the group. If he simply says yes but doesn't volunteer more, continue.)

"Well, as you probably know, RCEP has a simple mission: we believe that environmental protection is a religious issue and that people of faith need to speak out against environmental destruction. We work with a nationwide coalition of environmental groups to bring a liberal religious voice to the environmental debate."

(If the prospect says he hasn't heard of the group, state the information in the preceding paragraph and offer one or two specific examples of what you do. For example:)

"Our organization got Big Polluter Industry to install scrubbers on their chimneys, which reduced smog in our community significantly. This directly helped people with asthma and other respiratory illnesses, as well as those of us who would rather breathe clean air. The CEO of that corporation is a member of a church, and we were able to persuade him that his business practices were contradictory to his religious beliefs."

(*Pause* briefly, so that the prospect can comment if he wishes. If he doesn't, ask, "Are there any questions about our group I can answer for you?" or "Does that strategy seem good to you, Mr. Smith?" *Pause and answer questions.*)

(If Mr. Smith seems to agree with your group, then continue by saying:)

"I won't take up your time telling you all that we've accomplished—let me just tell you why I'm calling. Tonight we're looking for one hundred new members. If you give $35 or more tonight, you'll get our newsletter and a copy of our booklet 'And God Saw That It Was Good,' which is about the religious environmental movement. Will you help us with a gift of $35, $50, or $75?"

(*Pause.* If he agrees, arrange to get the money either with a credit card or a check. If he says, "$35 is a lot," tell him he can pay it in two installments. If he says he'd like to give $50 or $75, tell him what he gets for those amounts (if anything). If he says $35 isn't possible, tell him that you have other membership options and ask what he would like to give. Thank him for whatever he decides to do.)

Have participants note that the script is very respectful. Respondents are asked if they have time to talk at the very beginning of the phone call. They are asked what they know about the group and if they have any questions. The script is very short and to the point. Participants should also keep in mind that they are calling people who have some knowledge of their organization or some belief in their issue. They are using a process for finding names similar to the one described in the session on direct mail.

Preparing for a Phone-a-Thon, Continued   (Presentation; 15 Minutes)

After discussion of the script, continue with the final two steps to prepare for the phone-a-thon.

5. Prepare three letters for the callers to use and return cards and return envelopes to accompany them. One letter thanks the donor for making a gift of $___ (the caller fills in the blank). The second letter thanks the person for talking to the caller and includes more information about the group. The third letter is for people who weren't home; it also includes information on the group or the project. The return cards should have a place for the caller or the donor to specify how much the donor is giving.

6. Prepare a list of frequently asked questions and answers about your group for each caller to use. The most frequent questions and answers are:

- "What's your budget?"
- "Where do you get your money?"
- "Who is on your board?" or "Who's involved in this group?"
- "What do I get for my gift?"
- "Are you a nonprofit?" or "Is my gift to you tax-deductible?"
- "How can I get involved?"
- "How did you get my name?"

For religious groups, questions might also include:

- "Are you affiliated with one denomination?"
- "Are you funded by a church (or synagogue, or the Vatican, or other major religious institution)?"
- Depending on what religious tradition you are, people may ask further questions or make further comments about such figures as the Dalai Lama, Mother Teresa, the Pope, or local, well-known religious people. You're not required to agree or disagree or enlighten callers on things you don't know about or that are not related to your group.

The Evening of the Phone-a-Thon

On the evening of the phone-a-thon, callers should get together at least thirty minutes before the phoning begins. Go over the script and the frequently heard questions, and make the callers practice with each other. Do not skip this step. Be sure to have food for your callers and try to make the phone-a-thon festive.

The volunteers should be prepared for the fact that only five of every one hundred people called make a gift. Most are not home, some don't give money over the phone, some will be rude, and some engage in pleasant conversation but don't make a gift.

After the Phone-a-Thon

After the phone-a-thon, be sure to thank all the callers with a letter. Give them the results of the evening: how many people gave, and how much was raised over all?

Phoning After a Mail Appeal

Another way to use the phone is to follow up a mail appeal with phone calls to those who haven't responded. This method increases the response to the mail appeal. Here's how it works. Two weeks after a mail appeal goes out, everyone who has responded is taken off the list; those who haven't responded are called. The script varies slightly from a regular fundraising phone-a-thon in that a sentence is added to refer to the mail appeal, such as, "I'm Jean Vasquez from St. Cuthbert's Women's Shelter. We recently sent you a letter about our work. Did you have a chance to read it?" If the person has read it, you can move right to the close: "Will you be able to help us with a gift of $35 tonight?"

On the other hand, if the person can't remember the letter or claims not to have gotten it, the caller goes into a fuller description: "If you'll give me a few minutes right now, I'll tell you what it said."

Do's and Don'ts

There are a number of common mistakes that people involved in phone-a-thons make. We can avoid them by thinking about them ahead of time. Here they are:

- Don't ask emotionally charged leading questions that have only one answer ("Do you know that God loves retarded children?" or "Would you wish we had fewer children killed by guns in our community?"). These questions serve to make a person feel guilty, scared, or patronized. They are the common tool of some telemarketers. Although many people give money one time from guilt, shame, fear, or greed, they won't give a second time because they don't like being made to feel bad.
- Don't use a really long script, and do pause for breath while you're reading the script. Your script should be a few short sentences and should get to the point quickly. If you're describing something that is complicated to explain, punctuate your script with questions such as "Did you see the article about that in the paper last week?" or "Do you know about our group? I don't want to tell you things you already know."
- If the prospect says he doesn't give by phone but would like to see some information, don't assume he's just trying to put you off. Many people do not give to a stranger on the phone,

but that doesn't mean they won't give at all. Send them your literature.

- Do send follow-up letters and thank-you notes immediately. Thank-you notes with return envelopes should be sent the night of the phone-a-thon, or at the latest the next day.

Sample Script   (Work Alone and in Pairs; 20 Minutes)

Give participants ten minutes to work alone creating a script that is appropriate to their group, based on the sample script in their workbook. Point out that all they have to fill in are the name and mission of the group, a sentence or two about how they got started, and a sentence or two about their current work (pages 50–51 in their workbook).

Have participants form pairs sitting back-to-back or in some way so that they cannot see each other. Assign the person whose first name is closer to A in the alphabet to be the first solicitor. Tell everyone that on behalf of their group they are calling a person who gives to a similar group. They will be asking that person to consider joining the caller's group. The person playing the prospect is to give the solicitor time to go through the script.

Give each person two minutes to complete his or her call. At the end of two minutes, everyone switches roles.

Call everyone back together and ask what they learned by doing this exercise that they want to remember when they do this in real life. Responses are typically along these lines:

- Be prepared.
- It wasn't as hard as I thought it would be.
- I talked too much.
- I have to get to the point.

Ask if anything happened for which they would like the group's help in thinking of a response. If nothing comes up, ask them to consider what to do if:

- The prospect says he doesn't like the clergy person at your house of worship
- The prospect says she'd like to visit your program
- The prospect keeps asking a lot of questions and you want to end the phone call

Apart from being deliberately rude, there are no wrong approaches to answering these questions. Stress that the same questions or situations the caller might encounter while phoning for other reasons can arise while telephoning for money. In other words, nothing will happen to them on the phone when asking for money that might not happen otherwise.

Homework

Refer to the homework assignment, which is to find and write the answers to frequently asked questions for your group and to reflect on their feelings and attitudes about fundraising by phone.

Wrap-up

Many people who have done a lot of fundraising feel that raising money by phone is the hardest strategy. Others find that raising money by phone is fun and easy once they get into the rhythm of it. Once the participants are comfortable with this method, they will be comfortable with all the other strategies.

Raising money by phone prepares us for the next strategy: raising money from people we know by asking them in person.

Key Learnings

1. _____

2. _____

3. _____

Evaluation

Did the session meet its goals?

SESSION 11   *   *   *   *   *   *   *   *   *   *

Planning Major Gifts Campaigns

OVERVIEW OF SESSION

Goals   At the end of this session, participants will:

1. Be able to plan a major gifts campaign for their organization
2. Be able to identify a prospective major donor
3. Understand how to create and use a gift range chart

Methodology   Presentation, pairs work, discussion, role play

Time   One hour to prepare, one hour to present

Notes
- This session contains a lot of information, which you need to be as familiar with as possible.
- Photocopy the templates of a prospect list (Table 11.1, which is also in the participant's workbook, page 54) and gift range chart (Table 11.3), so that everyone has extras.
- The gift range chart (template in Table 11.3; sample chart in Table 11.2) often seems difficult to understand at first; try creating such a chart on your own a few times so you will feel comfortable answering questions about it.

- You may wish to create a template of the gift range chart (Table 11.3) on the flipchart ahead of time.

SESSION 11

Content

WELCOME EVERYONE to this session. See if there are questions or comments left over from the last session. If anyone missed that one, ask the group to summarize the key points.

Ask if anyone was phoned by an organization for a gift since the previous session, and how well the phoner did. Have participants' attitudes toward using the phone changed at all as a result of the last session?

Once everyone is settled, begin with a presentation.

Introduction to Major Gifts
Fundraising   (Presentation; 10 Minutes)

We've spent the past several sessions learning about various ways to ask for money. We've learned when to use special events, how direct mail works, and how the telephone can be an ally in our efforts. But in study after study, in recalling the most recent donation they made, when people are asked "Why did you make this gift?" 80 percent say, "Because someone asked me." Only 50 percent of those people can remember the organization they gave to, but 90 percent can remember who asked them. Even if the person was a stranger who came to the door, they remember what she looked like, or how polite she was, but they may well forget what cause the person represented.

Asking in person, then, is our best bet to get any money at all. Further, as the size of gift we seek increases, we finally get to the point where asking in person is the only chance of getting the gift. Few people—and probably none that we will ever meet—give $2,500, $5,000, or $10,000 by mail or phone. So if we want to move out into the world of major gifts, we must use personal solicitation.

From the donor's point of view, being asked in person is the most flattering of all strategies, the one that most involves the donor in the process of asking for the money.

In this session, we cover the first two of the three elements of major gifts fundraising:

1. First, who are we going to ask?
2. Second, how much are we going to ask for?
3. Third, how shall we ask?

Let's spend twenty minutes on each of these elements.

Personal Experience   (Discussion; 5 Minutes)

Ask participants how many have been approached for a large (whatever they define as large) amount of money in person. What was it like? Note how many fewer people have had the experience of being asked for money in person compared to being asked at a special event, phone-a-thon, or by mail. Point out that this lack of familiarity is part of what makes thinking about asking for money hard; you have little experience of your own to which it can be related.

Who Are We Going to Ask?   (Presentation; 10 Minutes)

Recall what percentage of response can expected when asking someone for money in person: 50 percent, with 50 percent of the people who give money giving less than what's requested.

Therefore, in soliciting gifts in person, we need four prospects for every gift. Two of them say no, one gives less than we ask for, and one person gives the gift we want.

Of course, these aren't just four random people. They've been identified as prospects. We've used the word quite a bit, so it's time for a formal definition. A prospect is someone about whom we know three things, which can conveniently be remembered as A, B, and C.

Write *ability, belief,* and *contact* on the flipchart; then go over each one, making additional notes as you wish.

1. *Ability*: evidence that a person has the ability to make a gift of the size you want

2. *Belief*: evidence that a person believes in your cause or shares your spiritual or religious values

3. *Contact*: evidence that a person knows someone in your organization, so you can establish contact with the prospect

Now take the participants through these criteria.

Contact

Because the most important factor is contact, let's start there.

If you don't know the person or don't have access to him, then you have a stranger and not a prospect. That's why you start with who you know.

Write this list on the flipchart:

Who Qualifies as Contacts of Yours?

- People you know personally
- People who are known by people you know
- People who are currently donors

The first item is self-explanatory. As for the people who are known by people you know, you might gain access to a person in this category by using the name of someone you both know.

Regarding current donors, though you may not personally know each current donor, you can call any donor and say, "We don't know each other, but we have in common that we support Verygood Group." Many of your best contacts are going to come from people who give money already.

Ask participants to compare the process of establishing a contact with any other form of networking. They, or you, might mention that this process is how people get jobs, how they find child care workers or plumbers, how they decide whether to explore a particular house of worship, and how they assess the idea of living in a particular neighborhood.

Determining Belief

Once you've established that you have some kind of contact with a person, then you look at what she believes in.

Ask yourself if there is any reason that the potential prospect would not believe in your organization. Groups working in a religious setting often think that a person won't believe in their cause for any number of reasons, especially if he's not of the same faith or of any faith. In fact, many prospects have no opinion one way or the other. Even people who are not of your religious persuasion may support some of the good work you do. A great deal of money is lost through assuming lack of belief on the part of a potential prospect.

More often, belief can be uncovered by bringing the cause closer to the prospect's personal experience. For example, an outreach ministry to homeless people has a faithful donor who is a successful computer consultant. She was homeless for one year some time ago. She volunteered to help with fundraising and told her story to several people in her church, one of whom has been vocally opposed to this ministry. On learning that his friend had at one time been homeless, he made a generous gift, accompanied by a note, "I had no idea that someone I know and respect could ever have been homeless. Her story has allowed me to change my opinion about homelessness and its causes." Certainly the power of the testimonial is familiar to almost all religious traditions, and people are usually much closer to many religious traditions than they think.

Once you've established that you know the person, or know someone who knows him, and that he has values or experiences similar to yours, you are ready to look at his ability.

Ability

The final characteristic of a prospect is ability to contribute. The first question to ask about ability is not how much money the prospect has, but whether he gives away money at all. Many people believe in feeding the hungry, visiting prisoners, or clothing the naked, but they don't make financial contributions to groups who are doing those things. Mother Teresa used to say, "Some people talk about hunger, but they don't come and say, 'Mother, here is five rupees. Buy food for those people.' But they can give a most beautiful lecture on hunger." People who are not givers are not prospective givers either.

Ability   (Brainstorm; 5 Minutes)

Ask the group to think about their friends and acquaintances. Do they know if any of them give away money? If they do, how did they find out? Record these answers on the flipchart.

Answers may include:

- We talk about groups we give to.
- I've seen their bumper stickers, refrigerator magnets, and newsletters.
- I've asked them for money.
- They've asked me for money.

- I've seen their name in another group's newsletter.

- They're active in their religious institution.

Ask the group, "Using the information generated here, how could we be more proactive with friends to find out if they give away money?"

Answers are likely to include:

- Talking about groups I give to and asking my friends how they make their giving decisions

- Paying more attention to things my friends tell me, such as that they're going to a board meeting or have attended a special event

- Asking about their bumper stickers, refrigerator magnets, or newsletters

- Asking them for a gift

The important thing to realize is that if:

- You know someone, and

- You know they give away money to charity, and

- You know they have similar values to yours

then the question is not "Should I ask them?" but "What should I ask them for?"

How Much Are We Going to Ask For?
(Individual Work, Discussion; 10 Minutes)

Ask participants to open their workbooks and turn to the template for creating a prospect list (Table 11.1 on page 54). Start with the first column. Have participants take two minutes to write down the names of people they know who know them—friends, relatives, neighbors, members of their congregation. Then ask them to make a note next to each name about their relationship with this person (friend, coworker, ex-husband, etc.). Now ask them to take only the people they both know and like, and who like them, and use the third column to note whether this person believes in the cause. Now take the people who have positive marks in all categories (the participant knows and likes him, he likes the participant, he believes in the cause) and make a note as to whether the prospect gives away money. By now, participants should have the idea.

Suppose they start off with the names of fifteen people they know. They are in a good relationship with twelve of them, of whom nine believe in their cause or share their values. Of those nine, the participant knows for a

TABLE 11.1

Template for Prospect List

Name	Relationship	Believes in Cause?	Gives Money?	Ask for How Much?
1.				
2.				
3.				
4.				
5.				
6.				
7.				
8.				
9.				
10.				
11.				
12.				
13.				
14.				
15.				

fact that five give away money; the rest she has questions about. But on the list next to those five people, the participant can write an amount of money they could be asked for.

> If you know someone, you know she gives away money, and you know she cares about your cause, then the question is not "Should I ask her?" but rather, "What should I ask her for?"
> The point of this prospect identification exercise is that you're not going to ask every person you know, or even every person you know and like. But you start with who you know and you end with the question about whether these people give away money.

The concept of starting with who you know rather than starting with who has money is fundamental to good fundraising. Fundraising is built around relationships, not money. People give because they care about the cause, or the person asking for the gift, or both, not because they have money.

Creating a Gift Range Chart   (Presentation; 15 Minutes)

The question of what you should ask them for brings us to the next part of this session, which is creating a gift range chart. In Session 13, we talk specifically about setting goals and creating budgets, but for now we need to focus on our major gifts goals.

Over the years, fundraising experts have observed the range of gifts that come into organizations and noted a pattern:

- A few people give large donations.
- Most people give much smaller amounts.
- There are some people in the middle who give donations that are not small, but not large either.

Using this pattern, it's possible to plan how many gifts, and of what size, we need to meet any fundraising goal. Once we know the number of gifts we require, we can plan how many prospects we have to contact for that number of gifts.

The pattern looks like this:

- About 50–70 percent of an organization's income comes from 10 percent of its donors.
- About 15–25 percent of the organization's income comes from 20 percent of its donors.
- The remaining 15–25 percent of the organization's income comes from 70 percent of its donors.

In other words, you will get a great many small gifts, but most of your income will be from a few large donations.

A second observation concerns gift size. Generally, for a campaign to be successful, this is the distribution of gifts you seek:

- One gift equal to 10 percent of the fundraising goal
- The next two gifts, in descending order of size, equal to the next 10 percent of the goal

- The next three to five gifts equal to an additional 10 percent of the goal

   After this top 30 percent, there are a greater number of gifts in lower amounts as we go down the chart. Let's illustrate these generalizations with an example.

Using the flipchart, write up the key points given here, and talk the participants through them.

   A synagogue wants to raise funds to assist other synagogues and churches that have been burned or vandalized in acts of racist or anti-Semitic violence. The fundraising goal is $100,000.

   This money will be raised using variety of grassroots strategies, including a mail campaign to the members of their congregation, special events involving the whole community, and a major gifts campaign seeking gifts of $250 or more. According to the general principles we've outlined above, then, here's how the income is expected to come in:

   - $50,000-$70,000 (50-70 percent of the money) comes from 10 percent of the donors, in gifts of $250 or more.
   - $15,000-$25,000 (15-25 percent of the money) comes from 20 percent of the donors, in gifts of $50 to $249.
   - $15,000-$25,000 (15-25 percent of the money) comes from 70 percent of the donors in small gifts of all sizes, but mostly $1 to $49.

   Knowing that they need to raise $50,000-$70,000 from their major gifts campaign, they compromise on the middle figure of $60,000 and create a chart to help them do that.

Write the gift range chart (Table 11.2) on flipchart paper, and explain each aspect of it.

Common Questions About the Gift Range Chart

Q: Why does the ratio go down as the size of gift goes down?

A: Because many of these gifts come in as the result of people saying no to a higher gift but agreeing to a lower gift, and because the smaller the gift, the more likely a person is to say yes to it.

Q: How do you know how many smaller gifts to project?

A: You can't be exact about these numbers, but because 10 percent of your donors are major donors, and the remaining 90 percent are midrange

TABLE 11.2

Sample Gift Range Chart

Gift Amount	Number of Gifts	Prospect-to-Donor Ratio	Number of Prospects Needed
$6,000 or more	1 (10 percent)	4:1	4
$3,000–$5,999	2 (10 percent)	4:1	8
$2,000–$2,999	3 (10 percent)	4:1	20
$1,000–$1,999	10	3:1	30
$500–$999	20	3:1	60
$250–$499	88	2:1	176
Total major gifts = $60,000	124		298

and smaller donors, take the number that 10 percent represents and figure out how many 90 percent would be. In the example of the synagogue, 124 people (10 percent) are major donors, so about 250 are midrange donors (124 times 2 = 248) and about 850 are small donors (124 times 7= 868).

Comments on the Gift Range Chart   (5 Minutes)

Don't be rigid in using this chart. It's more like a map drawn free-hand to help a friend find your house than a blueprint for construction. Your chart will vary from the sample work here, depending on the size of your community, the size of your lead gift (if you have someone give you 20 percent of your goal, you don't need as many small gifts) and the number of fundraising strategies you decide to use. On the other hand, this chart is useful; it indicates about how many gifts, and of about what size, you're going to need. The chart is a map, not a doodle.

Table 11.3, at the end of this session, is a template for the gift range chart.

Ask the participants how they think the gift range chart could be useful. Answers may include:

- It breaks the whole thing down into imaginable numbers.
- If we don't have prospects for our biggest gifts, we have to lower the goal.
- It helps with planning the campaign, and then evaluating it.

- We could show it to donors so they can see the rationale for setting gift amounts.

Trying It Out   (Pairs, Discussion; 10 Minutes)

Ask participants to assemble in pairs and create the top three rungs of a gift range chart for the fundraising goal for their project, using the template in their workbooks (p. 57).

Bring the group back together, and ask if there are any questions or places where people are getting stuck. Don't let the discussion get side-tracked into the math of the chart, or into a lot of detail. Emphasize that the gift range chart is to be used as a planning mechanism—it is not a blueprint. Conclude the exercise with these comments:

> The chart narrows the range of gifts you're seeking. If you don't know very much about a person's giving history, you won't start by asking for the biggest gift you need. Start by placing *yourself* on your gift range chart. What will you give? This helps you place your friends (who should be asked for gifts similar to yours, unless you have reason not to do that).

Reflection   (Discussion; 5 Minutes)

Ask people to reflect again on some of the prospects they were thinking of earlier, and whether the chart helps them identify amounts they might ask their friends or acquaintances for. Help people evaluate how it helps and how it doesn't.

Note that in some faith traditions, it's not customary to ask for a specific amount of money. People working in those traditions need help determining how to indicate what size gift they might want. Here are some examples.

- "The fellowship and joy of this congregation help many of us get around spiritually during the week. I've decided that this congregation is as important to me as my car, so I'm giving the same amount I paid for my car. I'm hoping you'll think of your gift in similar terms."

- "This church is a place for me to get away to every week and feel renewed. So my gift is equivalent to what I would spend at a bed and breakfast for a weekend. I'm hoping you'll think of your gift like that."

- "We're hoping everyone will give an amount that is equal to 2 percent of their income or more."

Ask participants to think of other examples; write them on the flipchart.

Note: asking for a specific amount of money makes fundraising much easier for both the organization and the donors. The donors know exactly what you want, and you can easily keep track of how many gifts have come in at the levels you need. So unless it is really not acceptable in your religious tradition, try to get participants to understand why it is important to ask for specific amounts.

Wrap-up

In this session we have learned how to prepare for making personal solicitations, including how to know how much to ask someone for. In the next session, we move on to the actual solicitation experience. This is the third element we discussed at the beginning of the session: how shall we ask?

Key Learnings

1. _____

2. _____

3. _____

Evaluation

Did the session meet its goals?

TABLE 11.3

Template for Gift Range Chart

Gift Amount	Number of gifts	Prospect/ Donor Ratio	Number of Prospects Needed

SESSION 12 ✳ ✳ ✳ ✳ ✳ ✳ ✳ ✳ ✳ ✳

Approaching Prospects for a Major Gift

OVERVIEW OF SESSION

Goals

At the end of this session, participants will:

1. Know the various steps in approaching someone for a large gift
2. Have confidence from practicing how to ask for large gifts during role plays

Methodology

Presentation, working alone, group work, role play

Time

One hour to prepare, 90 minutes to present

Notes

- As in so many of the sessions, the role play is key; if you are pressed for time, it would be better to have participants read some of the material on their own than to skip the practice session.
- You need a breakout room or a hallway where one-third of the group can talk for a few minutes while the rest do something else.

SESSION 12

Content

WELCOME EVERYONE to this session. See if there are questions or comments left over from the last session. Take time to review concepts because the last session contained a lot of content.

Reassure people that if they didn't understand something, this is normal; being able to say that you understood everything from the last session would be unusual. If anyone missed the last session, ask the group to summarize the key points for that person. After everyone is settled, begin with a presentation.

Approaching the Prospect   (Presentation; 15 Minutes)

In the last session, we covered the first steps in developing a major gifts campaign and preparing to solicit major gifts in person. Now we are ready to look at the three steps in approaching the prospect:

1. A letter describing the program and requesting a meeting to discuss it further
2. A phone call to set up a meeting
3. The meeting itself, in which the gift is usually solicited

Obviously, if you're approaching your best friend (or your spouse), you can skip the letter, and perhaps even the phone call. In some cases the letter is enough, and there's no need for a phone call and meeting; in others a phone call alone suffices. Let's go over each of these parts.

The Letter

The letter you prepare is slightly different for prospects who have given to this group than for prospects who have not given up to now. The letter to prospects who have given before is the simpler one. In it, you:

- Thank the person for his support in the past
- Ask him to give the same amount or more again
- Describe some of your achievements in the past year and some of your future plans
- End by saying you will phone in a few days to talk about his gift

- If appropriate, offer to meet with him
- Enclose a stamped return envelope

Phoning and offering to meet with current donors tells people they're valued and helps build their loyalty to the organization.

Some things to keep in mind about letters to prospects you know who have not given before:

- These letters rest heavily on the amount of respect and affection the prospect has for you.
- They use the same tone and format you would use in writing to this person about anything else (that is, if you normally call her by her first name, do that in your letter as well).
- They let your friend know that you're a donor yourself. You don't have to say how much you give; just the fact that you give tells your friend that you are asking her to do only what you are already doing.

Letters to prospects you don't know personally should include these elements:

- Begin the letter with a reference to what you have in common ("Martha Oldfriend gave me your name").
- Go on to describe the work of the organization and ask to meet with the person.
- Indicate in the letter that when you meet, you will be asking for money. The letter can describe how much the organization needs and what kind of gift you hope the prospect will make.

In writing all these letters, remember that most people have a short attention span. The letter is meant just to raise the person's interest. The follow-up phone call or face-to-face meeting is the time to convince the prospect to give.

Here are two sample letters. The first is to a prospect known to the solicitor.

Dear Martha and Bill,

It was great to see you both at the dedication of the AIDS Memorial Garden. I felt so inspired by all the people who turned out, many of whom have helped make this garden a reality.

As you know, when the idea of the garden was first presented to our church, there were some who were opposed to participating. I think the process we went through, the dialogue about God and judgment and how to honor people, was very important to building a community of faith.

The AIDS Garden is part of our larger ministry to people living with HIV/AIDS, and it is about that ministry that I am writing today. Because you have been involved in the discussions at our church about this ministry, and have always supported it, I am hoping you will support it with a financial contribution.

I have given $250 and have committed myself to raise $2,500. I am hoping you can help with a gift in the range of $250, but I certainly do not expect you to make a decision about this based on this letter alone. I would love a chance to talk more with you about the ministry and get your feedback on our work as you see it from your involvement in the discussions about it at church.

I will call you in a few days to see when we might have a cup of coffee together.

Best wishes,
Mary

A letter to a prospect you don't know:

Dear Martha (or Dear Ms. Murphy),

You have been a regular participant in our retreats at the Vipassana Retreat Center over the past several years. We appreciate your presence and your generous financial support.

We hope that for you and for many others, the Retreat Center may be a place of refuge, where the pain of the world and in our own lives may be met with compassion and understanding. With a community of like-minded people, we can explore the liberating potential in the Buddha's teachings of insight meditation, mindfulness, and lovingkindness.

We would like to ask you to consider increasing your donation to $500 this year to help us keep our class fees low and our meditation retreats open to everyone regardless of income. Because this is a doubling of your previous gift, I would like to talk to you about it in person, and answer any questions you may have.

Although we don't know each other, I think we have in common a deep commitment to the Retreat Center. It will be my pleasure to meet you, if you have time. I'll call you in the next few days.

Thank you in advance for your help.

Sarah Trudell
Board member

Have participants note that the letters are very brief. They tell the prospect what will be requested, but they also show that a big gift is not something to be entered into lightly. Each letter is respectful and thanks them for what they have already done. The invitation is to give, but also to come into a closer relationship with the organization and the person making the request. Sometimes solicitors move too quickly into the solicitation without enough thought about why a person would make a large gift, or how the person would like to be approached. Throughout this process, the emphasis is on building a community of donors. The size of the gift is much less important than the donor's feeling good about his or her gift and how it was solicited.

Direct Mail vs. Major Donor Letter   (Discussion; 5 Minutes)

What are the differences between a direct mail letter and a letter to a major donor prospect?

Answers may include:

- Direct mail letter has to make the case and ask for the gift in the letter, whereas this letter simply declares the writer's desire to phone the prospect.

- This letter establishes a relationship between the prospect and the solicitor.

> The relationship-building letter helps the prospect feel inclined to listen to the pitch about the group. By contrast, the main feature of the direct mail letter is to establish that the person receiving the letter believes in the cause that's being written about.

This is a good time to step back from the major donor solicitation for a minute to reinforce for participants the fact that any fundraising strategy requires looking at the audience, to establish what is the best method of communicating the request for a gift. The more an organization can tailor its appeals to its different constituencies, the more loyal donors will be, and the more money the group will have.

The Phone Call   (Presentation; 2 Minutes)

> Now, let's move on to the phone call. There are two important points to remember:

- If you say you're going to call, call. Nothing loses the confidence of the prospect more than failure to follow up on what you say you're going to do.
- Rehearse the phone call beforehand to anticipate possible difficult questions or objections the prospect might have.

Practice Phone Call   (Pairs, Discussion; 15 Minutes)

Have participants form pairs. Tell them that the participant who is older goes first. He or she is the solicitor, and the other participant is the prospect. Describe the scenario:

> The solicitor has sent the prospect a letter. This conversation is the phone call following the letter.
>
> The solicitor knows the prospect slightly, and the prospect has given money to this group before.
>
> The solicitor is asking the prospect for a meeting in which he or she will be asked to double his or her previous gift.
>
> The solicitor has two minutes to try to get a meeting.

After two minutes, have the participants switch roles.

Then, after about five minutes, bring the group back together and ask people what they learned that they will want to remember for real life. Responses generally include:

- It's very important to listen closely.
- It's very important to be flexible and assertive.
- It's hard to say no to someone who knows someone I know and who is from a cause I like.
- Sending the letter ahead of time helps.
- Don't try to read between the lines of what the person is saying; take her statements at face value.

Reassure participants that the phone call is the hardest part of the solicitation process, and that any nervousness on their part is normal. Reassure them further that they never sound as nervous as they feel. Emphasize that it is imperative that the calls be made. For the next five minutes, have participants practice another call, either with the same partner or a new one. At the end of that time, ask if the second call seemed easier.

The Face-to-Face Meeting   (Presentation; 10 Minutes)

> The purpose of the face-to-face meeting is to ask for the money.
>
> It is actually not as frightening as it seems, for several reasons:

- The prospect knows from your letter or your phone call that you will be talking about his making a contribution.
- He has agreed to see you, so the answer to your request will not be an outright no.
- In fact, the prospect is obviously considering saying yes, or else he would not have agreed to meet.

As the solicitor, you must appear poised, enthusiastic, and confident. If you're well prepared for the interview, this isn't too difficult. Many times, board members and volunteers are afraid they won't appear knowledgeable about the organization. It's perfectly fine to bring along a staff member or someone who has been with the organization a long time to answer difficult questions. Sometimes going with a partner also helps you feel more relaxed. It's also OK to answer a question with, "I don't know, but I'll be glad to get you that information." There's no problem if the conversation goes off on a tangent, but you must keep bringing it back to the financial needs of the organization and the possible role of the prospect in meeting those needs.

During the conversation, help the prospect see that giving to your organization is a logical and natural extension of his interests and concerns. To keep the conversation going, ask the prospect questions such as "Do you agree with our approach?" "Did you see the article about us in last week's bulletin?" "Has Martha Oldfriend talked much about our organization?"

When you finally ask for the gift, look the prospect right in the eye and in a clear, bold voice say, "Can you help us with a $300 contribution?" or, "We are hoping you can give $500 to $1,000." Keep looking at the prospect and don't say anything after you have asked for the gift. It's the prospect's turn to speak. Although it may feel like a long time between your request and his response, it's really only a matter of a few seconds.

Responses   (Brainstorm; 5 Minutes)

Ask participants to brainstorm all the possible responses a prospects might have to the question, "Will you help with *x amount of money*?" Use the flipchart to record the answers. After you write down all the responses, go through each one and ask participants how they might handle such a response. Suggestions for you as the leader follow each response.

Responses may include:

Yes.

> Thank the prospect and ask, "How would you like to pay that?" As soon as you can after you leave, write a thank-you note.

I'll think about it.

> Say, "That makes sense" or "I can understand that." Ask if the prospect needs any more information to help in his thinking. Then set a time when the prospect will be able to give an answer. "How about it if I call you next week? Does that give you enough time?"

Not now.

> Ask if the prospect wants to pledge and pay later, or whether you can call in a few weeks or months to see if he can consider a gift then. "Not now" implies a yes at a future date. Just use courtesy and common sense to figure out how to proceed.

I have to talk to my wife (or husband, or partner, or accountant).

> Say, "I can understand that"; then ask if there's anything in particular this other party wants to know or any way you can be helpful in conveying the request. End with a sense of when the prospect will have time to talk with this other party and make a decision.

That's a lot of money.

> Simply agree. "It is a lot of money. That's why I wanted to talk to you about it in person." The prospect wants reassurance that your organization thinks the gift is big—the prospect is not saying no, or "I can't afford that much."

I can't give that much.

> This is very different from the preceding response because the prospect is saying yes, but not to the amount as you've presented it. First, tell the person you don't need all the money at once. Does she wish to pledge over time? If not, then ask what gift she feels comfortable giving. Thank her sincerely for whatever amount she gives.

I still don't quite understand what you want to do.

> Go back to your case and see where the confusion is. Try to fig-
> ure out what the prospect needs to know at this point. Don't
> become impatient.

Come back to me when you have raised more money.

> Here's another yes disguised as a challenge. The prospect wants
> reassurance that you'll raise the money you need—she is not say-
> ing she objects to the gift you asked for or your cause. Ask if she
> wishes to make a challenge gift (agreement to a challenge would
> take the form, "I'll give $2,500 once you've raised $10,000"). If
> no, ask what amount the prospect would like to see in hand, and
> offer to return when you have that amount. Again, don't be impa-
> tient or seem in any way critical or disappointed by this decision.

Help participants see that none of the prospect's responses are rude or
hostile. Even if the prospect ultimately says no, you have had a chance to
talk about your work, which is always a good thing.

Practice Solicitation
(Small Groups, Role Play,
Discussion; 20 Minutes)

Ask the participants to count off into threes, remembering their own number and who the other two people are in their threesome. Tell them that person number one is a board member, number two is a staff member, and
number three is a prospect.

While persons one and two work together to develop their case, all the
threes go into another room. Each pair of persons one and two has to decide
how much to ask for, which person will do the final ask, and what things
they most want to present from their case. Meanwhile, the threes should
think about what they want to know if they are asked for a really large gift.
As much as possible, they should play themselves, but as people able to
give whatever they are asked for.

After five minutes, bring the threes back in and have the trios assemble
again. Allow seven minutes for the solicitation to take place, with both person one and person two participating in making the case to the prospect
and asking for a gift.

Reconvene the large group, and ask people what they learned from this
experience. Answers are likely to include:

- Be prepared.

- Having someone else there helps.

- It wasn't as scary as I imagined.
- It's flattering to be asked for a large amount of money.
- Enthusiasm is as important as having the facts.
- It's important to divide up the solicitation so that one person doesn't do all the talking.
- Know who is going to ask.
- Ask questions of the prospect—don't just talk.

Ask if participants feel they could now go and approach someone in person for a large gift. Ask those who feel they can't or that it would be hard to reflect on what would stop them. In the whole group, try to help each other get over any obstacles that remain.

Homework

Before the next session, ask one person for a gift for your group. It doesn't matter how much money, and it doesn't matter who it is; it can be the easiest person you can think of, and it can be a small amount of money. The point is to practice and to come to the next session with a real and recent experience of asking.

Wrap-up

Review the points that in our imagination, asking for money is much more frightening than doing it in real life. The key is to be prepared.

The people we ask for money are going to give it away to some group or other. We are simply saying that since they are going to give away the money, how about giving it to us?

Next session: setting goals and creating budgets. Explain that for the final sessions, we focus on the nitty-gritty details of planning, budgeting, and putting it all together. Ask participants to bring in the budgets they were given for the session on completing the case statement.

Key Learnings

1. _____
2. _____
3. _____

Evaluation

Did this session meet its goals?

PART THREE ✳ ✳ ✳ ✳ ✳ ✳ ✳ ✳ ✳ ✳

Creating a Fundraising Plan

THE TEST of all you have been learning and teaching is its usefulness for your work. In these final two sessions, you take participants first through the process of budgeting and then putting everything together into a fundraising plan. The latter can try the patience of a saint, and some tension is likely as participants work their way through this material. They may take out their tensions on each other, on a scapegoat, or on you. Knowing that this may happen helps you not respond defensively.

A strategy to deal with the tedium of creating a budget without resorting to shortchanging the process is to have two or three people do a lot of the work ahead of time, so that the group is not starting from scratch. You can always default to this suggestion if the group comes to an impasse.

On the other hand, some participants love these two sessions. They are nearly at the end, and they can see the applicability of all that they have learned. I hope this is your experience as the leader.

If your organization has had a good track record of budgeting and keeping track of expenses and income, you may wish to redesign the sessions slightly, leaving out some of the planning process and focusing on choosing new strategies for fundraising. By now, you should be comfortable refining the sessions to make them work best for you.

ABOUT GRADUATION, OR: A CLOSING RITUAL

Since participants have worked together over a period of many hours—whether you did this as weekly sessions or over the course of a weekend—

133

it is very nice to acknowledge how much work everyone has done. You may want to print up simple certificates of participation, or invite a member of the clergy or other leader to give a graduation talk on the importance of the work you have been doing. Many organizations find it helpful to make a plan for a reunion or for keeping their group going. You may even want to start exploring other fundraising strategies and design some of your own sessions.

The end of this course is just the beginning of ever-greater fundraising success for you and your organization.

SESSION 13 ✳ ✳ ✳ ✳ ✳ ✳ ✳ ✳ ✳ ✳

Creating a Budget

OVERVIEW OF SESSION

Goals At the end of this session, participants will:

1. Understand how to project expenses and income for their project or organization

2. Know from practice how to create a budget for a real project

3. Be familiar with the steps required to raise money for the project

4. Understand that raising money requires specific goals and time frames

5. Understand that the first step in developing a fundraising plan is developing an overall budget

6. Have a rough draft of a budget for their organization

Methodology Presentation and discussion, worksheets, small-group work, individual work

Time Forty-five minutes to prepare, 60–90 minutes to present

Notes
- Photocopy enough budget forms (Exhibit 13.1 in the participant's workbook) so that participants have two or three copies they can use for drafts.

- The length of this session depends on how much time you allow people to debrief their asking experiences from the previous session and how much work has been done on budgeting prior to this session. You may wish to allow the maximum amount of time and then let people go early if the session is completed quickly.

SESSION 13

Content

WELCOME EVERYONE to this session. Ask if there are questions or concerns about what was covered in the previous session. If anyone missed that session, ask participants to summarize the key points.

Sharing   (Discussion; 10 Minutes)

This exercise allows participants to debrief and share what they learned in the homework exercise. People will probably have learned a number of things. Your job as leader is to validate what people say and let them see that asking for money is possible, is not horrible, and may be pleasant.

Ask participants to tell each other about their experience asking for money. Do not focus on whether the participants were given the money or not. Emphasize that they were successful if they asked and unsuccessful if they did not. How did the practice session help them prepare for the solicitation? What else did they learn? For those who did not ask, make doing so their homework for next time.

Introduction   (Presentation; 1 Minute)

You're now in the final stretch. You've covered the basics of fundraising and the key grassroots fundraising strategies. These final two sessions help you put all of your knowledge into a workable plan.

We're almost done with our work here. We have one more session after this. We've gone from the macro to the micro. With our first session we looked at fundraising in the whole United States, for all organizations. We end by creating a fundraising plan for our organization, using the principles and strategies we've learned. Fundraising plans are created to meet the financial needs of the organization. Therefore, before we can develop a plan to raise the money we need, we have to know how much money that is. So, we start this session by taking a stab at developing an organizational budget.

What Is a Budget?   (Brainstorm; 5 Minutes)

Ask participants to brainstorm definitions of *budget*; record what they say on the flipchart. Answers may include:

- What it is going to cost to do the work we want to do
- What we are supposed to spend
- A statement of income and expenses for a specific period of time
- Itemized columns of numbers that provide a look at the work of a group
- The plan for income and expenses, which you compare to what really happened so you can make adjustments

Now ask them to list the characteristics of a healthy budget. Answers may include:

- Income is the same as expenses or exceeds them.
- Expenses make sense.
- All the numbers are realistic.
- It's not too much bigger than the year before without a good reason.
- It's easy to read and understand.

Be sure the following points are covered:

- A budget includes income as well as expenses.
- It covers a specific period of time, usually one year.
- It's a planning document to compare against monthly or quarterly financial statements.

Two-Step Process   (Presentation, Exercise; 45 Minutes)

> In this session, we're going to create a rough draft of your organizational budget using a simple, two-step process. In the first step, we divide into two groups: one estimates expenses for one year and the other estimates income. In the second step, we come back together and compare our numbers, discussing the rationale we used to arrive at them. We'll see if the relationship between expenses and income is a healthy one—that is, are we planning to raise at least as much money as we're planning to spend?

Hand out the budget forms and sample items (photocopies of templates in Exhibits 13.1 and 13.2 in the participant's workbook pages 64 and 65) and divide the group into two teams. Explain that one purpose of beginning by estimating budget items is to raise questions that require further research.

Give the following directions to the team that is estimating expenses.

The process of figuring expenses must be done with great attention to detail. For example, when looking at the line item "Printing," think of all the elements of what will be printed: letters, envelopes, return envelopes, newsletters, fliers, and so on. "Printing" should also include the cost of design and production where appropriate, or be on another line of the budget. As an example, a "special event invitation" is at least four separate printed pieces: the outside envelope, the invitation, the return card, and the return envelope—and someone has to design each of these pieces and get them ready to be printed. Similarly, a special event such as a dinner has many expense items, from invitations to food and wine, decorations, and so forth.

Explain to the group that their job is to prepare three estimates of expenses:

1. Start with the barest minimum the organization needs in order to survive.
2. Next, devise a budget that shows the amount of money required if the organization has a truly adequate amount of funding.
3. Using these two sets of numbers as poles, arrive at a third estimate somewhere in between; this is the most realistic one.

Things for the group to keep in mind:

- Avoid the temptation to have the realistic numbers be simply equidistant from the two poles; think of what is most realistic for each item.

- Avoid the temptation to underestimate expenses; it is always safer to overestimate expenses.

Give these instructions to the team that is estimating income:

This team's job is to choose the fundraising strategies you think are appropriate to your organization or project and estimate how much income can be generated. You must keep track of how much money must be spent to raise the amount you're projecting; when the other team rejoins you, the expenses that you project have to be rolled into the expenses that they have projected on their own.

The income team's procedure is the same as that of the expense team. They should prepare three budgets:

1. The least amount you can raise with minimal effort

2. The most you can reasonably expect to raise

3. Comparing the two extremes, an income projection that feels realistic

Remind both teams that this process may require further research and will not be finished today. They should do their best and be as accurate as possible, but gathering the information that is missing is very helpful to creating a final budget. The purpose of this session is to get a feel for working on budgets, so that they have a better sense of what goes into creating an accurate budget.

Regardless of how small the number of participants, avoid the temptation to create the budget working as one whole group. That makes it too tempting to boost income projections and reduce expense items to get to a balanced budget. Having the planning done separately increases the likelihood that people will project accurately.

Give the two teams twenty minutes to create their budget drafts, and then bring them back together.

Reporting   (Discussion, Presentation; 20 Minutes)

Ask one volunteer from each group to present the drafts, recording them on sheets of flipchart paper as they do. If you prefer, have them write their projections on flipchart paper before the presentation.

Summarize the presentations with this chart, giving the totals of the six budgets created and the choices they imply (comparing and contrasting all nine possible combinations, that is, survival expenses and minimum income, survival expenses and likely income, etc.):

Expenses	*Income*
Survival	Minimum
Reasonable	Likely
Fully funded	Best case

In creating the final budget, you can choose from each of these columns the amounts that seem most reasonable and comfortable. For example, you may choose to project expenses at the survival level, while assuming income will be at the likely level. That way you should never fear a deficit.

What other combinations are obvious from the numbers?

Ideally, the reasonable expense total is close to or slightly less than the likely income total. Sometimes, the reasonable expense total is close to or slightly less than the minimum income projection. However, if the survival expense total is the same as the best-case income total, then you have to decide whether you can live with that, or whether you need to negotiate some numbers.

Begin reconciling the two sets of numbers. Begin by asking for any questions that the teams producing the estimates still have before the members can feel their figures are final. Maybe the expense group needs more information on costs. Maybe the income group needs to ask a professional fundraiser to review the income plans and give some tips. Ask one participant to keep a running list of missing information that has to be researched later.

Next, ask for any additional questions from the teams that would help them understand the numbers presented. Do not let the participants revisit every number; otherwise, the whole group will repeat the work that the teams just did. If the teams have done their jobs properly, the numbers should be relatively accurate.

> You are not making a final budget in this class. The point is to identify what the sticking points are, and agree to do more research.
>
> Also, the budget is not a set of rules—it's a projection. Every month or quarter, depending on how fast you spend money, you add up your true expenses and income and compare that to the budget. The budget is a guideline and a numerical expression of the objectives you create in developing your case statement.

At the end of the exercise, explain to the group that there must be a completed budget before the next session; determine with them how they want to proceed. It is quite likely that two people will have to volunteer to create a final budget and bring it to the next session. Ask them to bring enough copies of the completed budget for everyone next time. Make an agreement on how the budget is to be finalized.

Reflection   (Discussion; 5 Minutes)

Once the group has agreed on how the budget will be finalized, ask them to reflect on the *process* of creating it with this question: "What did you learn from this exercise that you will want to remember for creating or evaluating budgets in the future?"

Answers may include:

- It helps ground our plans in reality.
- It's hard to be realistic.

- This process forces us not to fudge the numbers too much.
- There's a lot more to the process of creating a budget than I realized.
- It was actually easier than I thought.
- It's not much different from running a household.

Once the brainstorming is finished, note that many of the questions that the people playing the role of prospect (in Session 12) put forward about the organization have to do with budgeting.

> A good budget can help inspire people in their fundraising. Look at how much work gets done on so little money! Look at all the sources of money we have, which means the community thinks we should exist! Look at how much work and how much money remains to be done and raised—yikes! Better get to work!

Thank everyone for their hard work, and remind them of the agreed-upon process to finish the budget.

Wrap-up

Remind everyone that next session is the last one. Participants should review their notes to see what questions and concerns remain unanswered or unaddressed. You may want your last session to be longer than the others so you can have some kind of closing ritual, or even a guest speaker. Some groups like to prepare certificates for graduates or have a celebratory dinner. Whatever you decide, announce it at this class so that people can plan for it.

The next and final session is on putting together a draft fundraising plan.

Key Learnings

1. _____

2. _____

3. _____

Evaluation

Did this session meet its goals?

SESSION 14 ✳ ✳ ✳ ✳ ✳ ✳ ✳ ✳ ✳ ✳

Putting It All Together in a Fundraising Plan

OVERVIEW OF SESSION

Goals
At the end of this session, participants will:

1. Understand how one hour of planning can save three hours of work

2. Feel ready to go out and raise money

3. Understand how what they have learned up to now fits together

4. Understand that planning does not take the place of doing

Methodology
Presentation and discussion, group work, individual work

Time
Thirty minutes to prepare, one hour to present, plus time for closing ritual or graduation

Notes
- Before the session, purchase a wall-size "Year-at-a-Glance"-type calendar to use in the last part of this session. Make sure it has a small square for every day of the year, as you will be marking off specific days.

- Make folders for everyone with what they have completed in these sessions. This may include a case statement, sample direct mail appeal letters, gift range chart, and budget.

- Make sure there are enough copies of the budget that was completed after the last session so everyone will have one.

- You may wish to design a closing ritual or graduation.
- You may wish to do a final evaluation.

SESSION 14

Content

WELCOME EVERYONE to the last session. If there is anyone who asked a prospect for money between this session and the previous one, let the person describe the experience. Once everyone has settled in, begin with the opening exercise.

Final Questions and Concerns   (Discussion; 15 Minutes)

Ask one participant to record notes on the flipchart; ask the rest what final questions and concerns they have from all the previous sessions. As the list is compiled, ask participants to answer the concerns raised, if they can. The recorder writes the answers next to the questions. Assure participants that, although there is a lot more to know about fundraising, they now know (or know where to find) answers to almost all their fundraising questions and concerns.

Common questions or concerns, with suggestions for response:

Where will we find the time to do this?

> Break the work down into tasks, and tackle one or two tasks each day or week. Don't overschedule or set goals that aren't realistic. Make sure you're not spending time on work that is not important.

How can we be sure we're setting accurate goals?

> We can't. The first year in which we set goals, they may not be accurate, but it's important to have some goal we are working for. In subsequent years, we can learn from our first year and become more and more accurate. Our ability to be accurate depends on keeping good records and doing good analysis.

How do we keep records on all this stuff?

> We need to make a commitment to write up notes of our meetings and to make copies of everything and keep them in one central place. (If your organization has an office, that solves some of

your record-keeping problems.) We need a good database that volunteers can use easily, and we have to factor into our work plan keeping records and recording what we learn.

How can we train other people in what we know?

Every one or two years, we can go through a course like this with a number of people. We can also do minitrainings on specific subjects. With good records, the learning curve isn't as steep because there's no recreating what happened. Training volunteers is part of our work and must be planned also.

Introduction   (Presentation; 1 Minute)

Now we move to the final piece of our training session: putting it all together in a fundraising plan. To get ourselves into the proper mind-set, let's start with a role play.

Destination Nowhere   (Role Play, Discussion; 7 Minutes)

Ask for two volunteers to come to the front of the room. Tell the group that one volunteer is a travel agent and the other is someone wanting to make travel plans. Whisper to the one wanting to make travel plans that she is to be as vague as possible—for example, not saying where she wants to go, only that she wants to go somewhere nice. She is not to say how much money she can spend, only that it's some money but not too much.

Give the role players two minutes to act out their roles. After two minutes, have them sit down and ask the class to comment on how watching the role play made them feel.

Answers may include:

- I felt very frustrated.

- I felt really sorry for the agent.

- Even if the agent suggested something, the customer wouldn't know if it was the right thing, because she didn't know what she wanted.

- If you don't know where you're going, any road will get you there.

The purpose of the exercise is to demonstrate how frustrating it is for donors if we're not specific about what we need—not only what our budget is, but also what we want from them. We must know what we want, why we want it, by when, and from whom. When we put all that together, we have a fundraising plan.

Creating a Fundraising Plan   (Presentation; 10 Minutes)

There are five steps in creating a fundraising plan:

Write the steps on the flipchart as you speak.

1. Create a budget. We did that in the last session, and we have the final budget today, so we can move to step 2.
2. Look at the amount of money that must be raised from individuals, and divide it as we learned to do in our session on major gifts:
   - About 50-70 percent of the money comes from major gifts, to make up 10 percent of our donors.
   - About 15-25 percent of the money comes from medium-sized gifts, to make up 20 percent of our donors.
   - The remaining 15-25 percent of our money comes from 70 percent of our donors, in small to medium-sized gifts.
3. Next, you look at each of these categories and see how many donors you already have in each one and how many more you must attract.
4. Match the number of donors required in each category with the strategies best suited to attracting them. Think about what you learned in Session 6 (the overview of fundraising strategies), and in the sessions on special events, direct mail, and personal solicitation (sessions 7-12).
5. Place steps 3 and 4 on a time line, and voilà: a fundraising plan! (See the example of Table 14.3 in the workbook.)

Creating a fundraising plan is one of those things that are easy to describe and a lot more work to do, so let's spend the rest of our session putting this plan together.

Steps Two Through Four   (Solo Work, Brainstorm, Small Groups; 35 Minutes)

Pass out the completed budgets from the last session.

Make three columns on the flipchart (or use three separate sheets of paper) as in Table 14.1: Major Gifts, Midrange Gifts, and Small Gifts.

Review how donations come into an organization:

- 50–70 percent is from 10 percent of donors.
- About 15–25 percent is from 20 percent of donors.
- The remaining 15–25 percent is from 70 percent of donors.

Instruct participants to work alone to fill in Table 14.1:

> Beginning with the total amount of income needed from individuals in your budget, divide it, using these percentages, into major gifts, midrange gifts, and small gifts and put the amount needed for each onto Table 14.1. We will come back to the columns for strategies in that table.

TABLE 14.1

Segmenting Your Donors

Major Gifts	Midrange Gifts	Small Gifts
Goal $_____ , from _____ donors	Goal $_____ , from _____ donors	Goal $_____ , from _____ donors
Strategies:	**Strategies:**	**Strategies:**

After ten minutes, continue with the next part of the exercise:

> Now, based on what you know about developing a gift range chart from Session 11 and the figures you have put in Table 14.1, create a Gift Range Chart, using Table 14.2. (You can refer back to page 56 in your Participant Manual for a sample gift range chart for a $60,000 major gift campaign in a $100,000 overall plan for raising money from individuals.) Going beyond major gifts, also determine the number of gifts and prospects your budget will require for gifts in the midrange and small categories.

TABLE 14.2

Gift Range Chart for Creating a Fundraising Plan

Major Gifts Goal: $_____

Gift Amount	Number of Gifts	Prospect-to-Donor Ratio	Number of Prospects Needed

Midrange and Small Gifts Goal: $_____

Gift Amount	Number of Gifts	Prospect-to-Donor Ratio	Number of Prospects Needed

After fifteen minutes, ask participants to bring their attention back, no matter how far they have gotten in their gift range chart. Take five or ten minutes to construct a collective Gift Range Chart based on participants' work alone, and put it on the flipchart for common reference. Try not to get bogged down at this point; the chart may need more work, but if it has the general categories of major, midrange, and small gifts and some idea of how many are needed in each, that will be a good start.

Ask participants to return to their copy of Table 14.1 and, using what they learned about what strategies are best suited to attracting donors in each category of giving, to note under each giving range in the table the strategies that will be used to attract donors in that range. Point out that with that information they can also complete the third and fourth columns of Table 14.2, Prospect-to-Donor Ratio and Number of Prospects Needed.

Next, ask the group to divide into small groups—one for each strategy—to plan more details of the strategies. Make sure the groups have roughly equal numbers of people and easel paper on which to write up their plans. There may not be enough groups to cover all the strategies.

In your small group, flesh out this skeletal plan, using Table 14.3. For example, if your strategy is "a special event," then decide what event and when it will be. If you list an actual event, such as an auction you do every year, then you must decide how to make it as effective as possible. Those of you in the major gifts group have to create, or refer to, the gift range chart, and begin to list prospects or sources of prospects.

As with the budgeting session, the goal is not so much to finish the fundraising plan as to understand and appreciate the process and feel able to do a more thorough job at another time. Any progress we make here will be very helpful in the future.

After fifteen minutes, call everyone back together and ask for a report from each group. Determine if there is consensus that the plans the small groups have made are adequate to proceed to the next step. That is, although the plans may be modified, there should be no major disagreements on types of strategy. If there are disagreements, decide on a process by which they can be resolved. For example, if the special-event group has decided to get rid of the annual auction and replace it with a movie benefit, while the major gifts committee is counting on the auction so they can give major donors a preview of the auction items as a thank-you gesture for their generosity, the whole group has to solve this problem.

If it seems that the disagreements can be settled in five minutes or so, allow the discussion to happen now. If it seems that more information or discussion is required, set up a process by which that will occur at another time.

Whether the group is in total agreement or not, ask them to act as though they are, to experience the final part of this planning process: putting together the time line.

Creating a Time Line   (Brainstorm; 20 Minutes)

Put the "Year-At-A-Glance"-type calendar you purchased on the wall (see the notes for this session) and ask the participants to fill in as much as possible.

Have them begin by marking any known events, including religious holidays, school holidays, and any other times many people will not be available. Most churches have to raise money on a nine-month year because the ministers are away for the summer and attendance is down. Campus ministries have to work around the school year. Tell participants to avoid the mistake of simply marking "Easter" or "Buddha's Birthday" or "Passover." Many religious holidays culminate on a certain day but with a period of ritual leading up to or following that day. The Days of Awe, Ramadan, and Lent are examples of fairly extended periods of time that will have some degree of impact on your organization, depending on how your religious group observes these times.

After these are recorded, have participants note any dates that are already in place for the group, including board meetings, retreats, and deadlines for such things as newsletter production and grant applications. Now, they can put everything that they have planned for fundraising into the remaining time. Again, this part of the planning will not be completed here.

Bring this exercise to a close in time to allow a final fifteen minutes for wrap-up. Ask participants what they learned by creating this fundraising plan and putting it on a calendar. Answers may include:

- There's a lot of checking and balancing in this process. At first it seems redundant, but then you realize that it's a good thing.

- I wish we'd known how to do this earlier; we would have saved a lot of time.

- This whole process forces us to be more and more specific, which is a lot of work.

- This process takes a lot of the anxiety out of fundraising and replaces it with plans. I guess that's the point.

Wrap-up

Ask participants to take two minutes to reflect in silence on the whole fundraising course and to think about these final questions:

- What are the key things you have learned?

- How is what you learned about fundraising helpful in your faith journey?

Ask them to get into pairs and share their thoughts for two or three minutes. After that time, bring them back together and ask for comments from the whole group on each question. If the comments in the following lists are not mentioned, you should mention them:

Key Ideas About Fundraising

- If you want money, you have to ask for it.

- If you ask enough people, using strategies appropriately, you will raise the money you need.

- We know a lot more about fundraising than we think we do, since so much of it is built around common sense, hospitality, and talking about ideas and values.

- Fundraising is formulaic. There are known things that work and known ways of planning; our job is to take that information and apply it to our group.

Key Ideas About Fundraising and the Faith Journey

- Asking people to give away money is a gift to them. It allows them to express their values.

- Asking for money reminds us that we have very little control over outcomes, but we can ask for what we want. The Creator wishes us to have what we need.

- When we give away money, we are only giving that which has been given to us. We are stewards rather than owners of our money.

Review with everyone what has been completed by the group (see the goals at the opening of this session).

Summarize any action steps for moving forward. If this group is to meet again, set that meeting and agenda.

Thank everyone for their attendance, participation, and hard work. Remind them that the real work of fundraising begins now that they have learned how to do and plan for it.

Call their attention to the Bibliography in the back of the participant's workbook.

Do the closing ritual, if you have designed one.

Do a final evaluation, if you have designed one.

Finally, keep these words from Martin Luther in mind as we close: "This life, therefore, is not godliness but the process of becoming godly, not health but getting well, not being but becoming, not rest but exercise. We are not now what we shall be, but we are on the way. This process is not yet finished, but it is actively going on. This is not the goal, but it is the right road. . . ."

* * * * * * * * * * * *

Bibliography

Other titles by Kim Klein (all from Chardon Press, Oakland, Calif.)

Fundraising for Social Change (4th ed. revised and expanded, 2000, originally published 1988). A complete guide to individual donor fundraising for grassroots nonprofits.

Fundraising for the Long Haul (2000). For older social change organizations exploring their particular challenges. Case studies, personal experience, and how-to characterize this book.

Getting Major Gifts (rev. 1999). Collection of twelve articles on developing major gifts, reprinted from *Grassroots Fundraising Journal*.

Other useful fundraising materials from Chardon Press

The Board of Directors. Collection of ten articles on creating and building an effective board of directors, reprinted from *Grassroots Fundraising Journal*.

Grassroots Fundraising Journal. Bimonthly how-to periodical.

Grassroots Grants, by Andy Robinson (1997). Hands-on guide to researching and writing grant proposals.

Inspired Philanthropy: Creating a Giving Plan, by Tracy Gary and Melissa Kohner (1998). A step-by-step guide in how to match your giving with your values.

Contact Chardon Press at 3781 Broadway, Oakland, CA 94612. Call 888/458-8588 (from the Bay Area, 510/596-8160), or visit www.chardonpress.com. The website is also designed to be a fundraising course on-line.

Additional fundraising materials from other sources

Achieving Excellence in Fundraising, by Henry Rosso and Associates (San Francisco: Jossey-Bass, 1990).

Beyond Fund Raising: New Strategies for Nonprofit Innovation and Investment, by Kay Sprinkel Grace, (New York: Wiley, 1997).

Effective Social Action by Community Groups, by Alvin Zander (San Francisco: Jossey-Bass, 1990).

Faith and Philanthropy in America, by Robert Wuthnow, Virginia A. Hodgkinson, and Associates (San Francisco: Jossey-Bass, 1990).

Giving USA: Annual Report on Philanthropy (Indianapolis: American Association of Fund Raising Counsel [AAFRC] Trust for Philanthropy, annual).

Giving USA 1999: The Annual Report on Philanthropy for the Year 1998, ed. Ann E. Kaplan (Indianapolis: AAFRC Trust for Philanthropy, 1999).

Grassroots and Nonprofit Leadership, by Berit Lakey, George Lakey, Rod Napier, and Janice Robinson (Philadelphia: New Society, 1995).

"Grassroots Fundraising: The Kim Klein Video Series" (Minneapolis: Headwaters Fund). Seven topics are covered in twenty-minute sessions in a professionally produced video series with accompanying workbook.

The Grassroots Fundraising Book, by Joan Flanagan (Chicago: Contemporary Books, 1992).

Holding the Center: America's Nonprofit Sector at a Crossroads, by Lester M. Salamon (New York: Nathan Cummings Foundation, 1997).

How to Produce Fabulous Fundraising Events: Reap Remarkable Returns with Minimal Effort, by Betty Stallings and Donna McMillion (Pleasanton, Calif.: Building Better Skills, 1999).

The Nonprofit Manager's Resource Directory, by Ronald A. Landskroner (New York: Wiley, 1996).

Raising Money by Mail: Strategies for Growth and Financial Stability, by Mal Warwick (Berkeley, Calif.: Strathmoor Press, 1994).

The Second Legal Answer Book for Nonprofit Organizations, by Bruce R. Hopkins (New York: Wiley, 1999).

Special Events: Proven Strategies for Nonprofit Fundraising, by Alan Wendroff (New York: Wiley, 1999).

Successful Fundraising: A Complete Handbook for Volunteers and Professionals, by Joan Flanagan (Chicago: Contemporary Books, 1991).

Successful Fundraising for Arts and Cultural Organizations, by Karen Brooks Hopkins and Carolyn Stolper Friedman (Phoenix: Oryx Press, 1994).

Organizations

American Association of Fund-Raising Counsel and
AAFRC Trust for Philanthropy
37 E. 28th St., Ste. 902
New York, NY 10016
212/481-6705
www.aafrc.org

The Chronicle of Philanthropy
1255 23rd St., NW, Ste. 700
Washington, DC 20037
202/466-1000
www.philanthropy.com

Contributions
P.O. Box 338
Medfield, MA 02052
508/359-0019
www.contributionsmagazine.com

Council for Advancement and Support of Education (CASE)
1307 New York Ave., NW, Ste. 1000
Washington, DC 20005-4701
www.case.org

Council on Foundations
1828 L St., NW, Ste. 300
Washington, DC 20036
202/466-6512
www.cof.org

The Foundation Center
79 Fifth Ave.
New York, NY 10003-3076
212/620-4230
www.fdncenter.org

The Fund-Raising School
Indiana University Center on Philanthropy
550 West North St., Ste. 301
Indianapolis, IN 46202–3162
317/274-7063
www.fcop.org

INDEPENDENT SECTOR
1200 18th St., NW, Ste. 200
Washington, DC 20036
202/467-6100
www.indepsec.org

National Catholic Development Conference
86 Front St.
Hempstead, NY 11550
516/481-6000
www.amm.org/ncdc.htm

National Center for Nonprofit Boards
1828 I St., NW, Ste. 900
Washington, DC 20036-5104
202/452-6262
www.ncnb.org

National Charities Information Bureau
19 Union Square West
New York, NY 10003-3395
212/929-6300
www.give.org

National Committee for Responsive Philanthropy
2001 S St., NW, Ste. 620
Washington, DC 20009
202/387-9177
www.ncrp.org

National Committee on Planned Giving
233 McCrea St., Ste. 400
Indianapolis, IN 46225
317/269-6274
www.ncpg.org

National Council of Churches of Christ in the U.S.A.
475 Riverside Dr., Ste. 850
New York, NY 10115-0050
212/870-2227
www.ncccusa.org

National Council of Nonprofit Associations Calendar
1000 L St., NW, Ste. 605
Washington, DC 20036
202/467-6262
www.ncna.org

National Society of Fund Raising Executives
1101 King St., Ste. 700
Alexandria, VA 22314
703/684-0410
www.nsfre.org

NonProfit Times
240 Cedar Knells Rd., Ste. 318
Cedar Knells, NJ 07927-1621
973/734-1700
www.nptimes.com

Philanthropic Advisory Service
c/o Council of Better Business Bureaus
4200 Wilson Blvd., Ste. 800
Arlington, VA 22203
703/276-0100
www.bbb.org

* * * * * * * * * * *

The Author

Kim Klein is internationally known as a fundraising trainer and consultant. She is the co-owner of Chardon Press, which publishes and distributes materials that help to build a stronger nonprofit sector. She is founder and copublisher of the bimonthly *Grassroots Fundraising Journal* and author of *Fundraising for Social Change* (now in its fourth edition). Her book is widely used by practitioners and students alike. It is required reading for nonprofit or public interest programs at the University of San Francisco, California State University-Chico, Harvard University, Southern Methodist University, Hunter College, University of Baltimore, Tulane University, and many more. Her most recent book, *Fundraising for the Long Haul*, explores the particular challenges of older grassroots organizations.

In addition to the writing she does for her own publications, she has contributed many articles to leading books and periodicals in the field of fundraising. Klein also has a popular video series on fundraising, distributed by the Headwaters Fund in Minneapolis.

Klein has worked in all aspects of fundraising, as a staff person, volunteer, board member, and consultant. She is best known for adapting traditional fundraising techniques—particularly major donor campaigns—to the needs of organizations with small budgets that are working for social justice. Widely in demand as a speaker, she has provided training and consultation in all fifty states and in sixteen countries. She was named Outstanding Fund Raising Executive of the Year in 1998 by the Golden Gate Chapter of the National Society of Fund Raising Executives.

She graduated with honors from Beloit College, majoring in religion and classics, and did graduate work at the Pacific School of Religion.